STOCK MARKET FOR BEGINNERS

THE ULTIMATE GUIDE TO CREATE A PASSIVE INCOME FOR LIVING. STRATEGIES TO EASILY AND PROFITABLY INVEST IN STOCKS, FOREX, SWING, OPTIONS, AND DAY TRADING

BY JOHN SCOTT

© Copyright 2019 - All rights reserved.

The content contained within this book may not be reproduced, duplicated or transmitted without direct written permission from the author or the publisher.
Under no circumstances will any blame or legal responsibility be held against the publisher, or author, for any damages, reparation, or monetary loss due to the information contained within this book. Either directly or indirectly.

Legal Notice:
This book is copyright protected. This book is only for personal use. You cannot amend, distribute, sell, use, quote or paraphrase any part, or the content within this book, without the consent of the author or publisher.

Disclaimer Notice:
Please note the information contained within this document is for educational and entertainment purposes only. All effort has been executed to present accurate, up to date, and reliable, complete information. No warranties of any kind are declared or implied. Readers acknowledge that the author is not engaging in the rendering of legal, financial, medical or professional advice. The content within this book has been derived from various sources. Please consult a licensed professional before attempting any techniques outlined in this book.

By reading this document, the reader agrees that under no circumstances is the author responsible for any losses, direct or indirect, which are incurred as a result of the use of information contained within this document, including, but not limited to, — errors, omissions, or inaccuracies

Table of Contents

Introduction: 6
Chapter 1: How to Get Started with Stocks 10
Chapter 2: Creating Passive Income with Dividend Stocks 14
Chapter 3: A Day Trading Strategy 19
Chapter 4: Create a Timeline for Systematic Investing 24
Chapter 5: Swing Trading Tactics 29
Chapter 6: Forex Trading Tactics 34
Chapter 7: Playing the Stock Market Through Mutual Funds 39
Chapter 8: Make sure you have the Right Tools to Trade Profitably 45
Chapter 9: Opening your Trading Account 50
Chapter 10: Choosing a Stock and What You Need for Trading 54
Chapter 11: How to Buy and Sell Stocks 59
Chapter 12: The Hidden Evils 64
Chapter 13: Masters Insight 68
Chapter 14: Advance Stock Market Strategies and Tactics 73
Chapter 15: Brokers and Platform of Trading 79
Chapter 16: Facts and Numbers to Help You 83
Chapter 17: Forex Vs. Stocks 88
Chapter 18: Finding a Suitable Market 92
Chapter 19: Stock Market Technical Analysis 97
Chapter 20: Pros and Cons 101
Chapter 21: The Fundamentals of the Stock Market 105
Chapter 22: Beginners Mistakes 110
Chapter 23: Mindset and Psychology 114
Chapter 24: Tips for Becoming a Successful Top Trader 119
Conclusion: 123

Introduction

People like to throw around the word stock. But most people don't understand what it means. For the record, let's clarify the meaning of the word so that you understand what you're getting into.

Stock is an ownership stake in a company. When a company issues stock, it divides up the ownership into portions called shares. You buy an ownership stake in a company by purchasing shares of stock. So, if you purchase shares of Exxon, which means that you are one of the owners of Exxon that entitles you too many things, including a share of the company profits. As the fortunes of the company improve, the value of the shares increases because there will be more demand for ownership. If the company experiences bad times, or the economy starts doing badly, investors will start selling off their ownership stakes. That means supply will exceed demand, causing prices to drop. Since owning shares in the company may not be seen as profitable, the prices have to drop to attract new buyers.

Publicly traded companies issue large numbers of shares, and they are traded on regulated public markets called stock exchanges. There are two general classes of stock. These are:

- Common stock: This is what most people are referring to when they use the word stock. A common stock gives you an ownership stake and voting rights in the company. Voting will occasionally take place when shareholders have the opportunity to vote on important company decisions. Shares of common stock entitle the holder to receive dividends. But not all companies pay dividends, as we'll explain in a moment. Something to keep in mind is that common stockholders are last in line if a company decides to liquidate or declare bankruptcy.

- Preferred stock: These are individual shares that are, in a sense, more like bonds. Preferred stock does not confer voting rights, but there are other advantages to owning the preferred stock. In some cases, companies will guarantee the yield paid with dividends. Preferred stock also confers some rights not available to common stockholders, such as being ahead of them in line when a company goes bankrupt. If a company goes under, creditors and bondholders will get paid first. Then preferred shareholders will get paid, and finally, if anything is left over, common stockholders get paid. Most companies don't issue preferred stock. Some companies in the financial sector, like Bank of America, offer preferred stock.

What is a Dividend

Many people invest in the stock market, hoping to earn income from dividends. However, it's essential to know that not all companies pay dividends. Let's explore how this works.

When a company earns profits, they have some choices. They can pay out all the profits to the owners, which are the shareholders. Or they can reinvest some of the money back into the company. That means they will build new plants, invest in research and development, or hire more employees. They may put a large sum of money behind efforts to break into a new market, such as entering a developing market for the first time.

Companies that are experiencing a rapid growth phase may choose to reinvest all of their profits back into the company. These companies do not pay dividends because all of their profits have been reinvested. Even though these stocks don't pay dividends, they may be highly prized. Examples include Amazon, Netflix, and Google. Investors seek out these stocks because they appreciate or gain value over time.

If a company pays dividends, it's more likely to be an older, more stable company. Examples include IBM and GE. That doesn't mean the company isn't growing; Walmart also pays dividends and continues to experience growth. But the company is more mature than a new company like Tesla, which is poised for rapid growth. The amount paid in dividends varies widely. Deciding what stocks to buy depends on what your investment goals are.

Preparation

Before quickly opening an account and starting to load up on stocks, an investor needs to put some effort into preparation. This will include three phases, and to be honest, preparation is a long-term effort. The first stage in preparation is to review your own personal situation thoroughly. You'll need to determine if you are ready for investing, and how much you need to invest. Simply knowing what your financial goals are is a large part of the process of preparation.

The preparation process will be ongoing. Before you invest in any stock, you will need to analyze the company and its past performance thoroughly. You'll need to determine how well any given stock fits in with your own financial goals, and square this with the prospects of the stock going forward. While you don't have to be a financial expert, it's essential to determine the prospects of any given company going forward. Sometimes you will make the wrong bets, but using the right strategies can help minimize your overall risk.

Preparation continues after you've invested in a company. You'll need to keep track of the stock and periodically evaluate its performance. At times, you may have to decide whether or not to keep a company in your portfolio. And you'll be picking new stocks to include in your investments. As an active investor, preparation is an ongoing process. People who enjoy financial analysis and business are the best suited for active investing.

Picking Winning Stocks

The million-dollar question is: knowing how to select winning stocks. While there are no guarantees in life, there are guidelines you can follow that will increase your odds of success. The fact is knowledge is power, and having some knowledge about how the stock market behaves and about the companies that you invest in will help you grow wealth over time.

There are several factors to consider when picking winning stocks. It's important to realize that you aren't always going to get it 100% right. Even the best investors make mistakes. The key to success is picking yourself up and moving on when mistakes happen and focusing on your overall portfolio rather than on individual wins and losses. Thinking long-term always helps as well.

Let's go over some of the critical points that are important when picking winning stocks.

Understanding Company Value

New investors may have a gut-level understanding that Apple and Google are valuable stocks. But it's essential to understand what makes a stock valuable. Investing in hunches can produce profits sometimes, but in most cases, it will lead investors sideways or even toward losses. It's essential to combine your gut-level feelings about different investments with the cold, hard facts that we can derive from doing analysis.

There are two types of analysis used by professional investors, fundamental analysis and technical analysis. Over the long-term, fundamental analysis is more important. This involves studying the company's "fundamentals" – profit margins, cash on hand, assets, liabilities, trends in revenue, products, and services the company is offering, and management. The company's plans and potential for the future also play a role in fundamental analysis. Companies that may not be profitable now may be secure investments because of the potential. For years Amazon didn't earn any profits, but investors knew it was disrupting the marketplace and was likely to become a giant. A disruptive technology might make a company well placed for future gains. An example of this is Tesla, which is currently going through some rough spots. But it may still be a good investment because over time the technologies the company is developing might turn it into tomorrow's Amazon.

The first way to assess company value is to look at its market capitalization. This is the number of outstanding shares multiplied by the current share price. So, if a company has 1,000 outstanding shares and they are trading at $20 a share, the market capitalization is $20,000. Companies with a high level of market capitalization tend to be more mature, stable, and dominant. They are poised to enjoy a stable long-term future that will bring investors good returns. Examples of companies with large market capitalization include Apple, Netflix, Walmart, and Google.

However, young companies that have lower market capitalization can be great investments as well. Smaller market capitalization is often a trade-off between risk and the possibility of substantial growth in the future. In the late 1990s, people who made that bet on Amazon when it was a relatively small and growing company have been paid handsomely for their decision. However, the risk can be high. There were many "dot com" companies around in the 1990s which seemed as appealing or more appealing than Amazon that don't even exist anymore. It's hard to know with any reasonable degree of certainty which smaller company is going to break out over time. That's one reason why diversity is essential, and we'll show you ways that you can take advantage of the growth that young and smaller companies may offer without putting your investments at risk.

Chapter 1: How to Get Started with Stocks

Some people like to buy stocks and hold them for many years. We call them "investors."

Other people like to buy and sell stocks more quickly, maybe holding them for only an hour, a day, a week, or a month. We call these people "traders."

Both are perfectly good ways to make money in the stock market. Some investors look down on traders, and vice versa. I would urge you not to take a side in this debate.

I am both a trader and an investor. I like to have many different strategies running at the same time: long-term strategies, short-term strategies, as well as strategies that involve bonds, options, futures, currencies, venture capital, and real estate. You should try the different strategies that I describe in this to discover what works best for you and your psychology and risk tolerance.

Remember to consult with a registered financial adviser before making any investment decisions.

Then when you are ready, the question will arise:

So how exactly do I buy a stock?

Stocks are usually bought and sold on what are called "stock exchanges." A stock exchange is simply a place where buyers and sellers show up and exchange their shares for money, or their money for shares. A stock exchange is a little bit like an eBay for stocks.

The most well-known exchanges in the U.S. are the New York Stock Exchange (NYSE) and the Nasdaq. The NYSE is best known for its blue chip (high-quality) stocks like Coca-Cola and McDonald's. The Nasdaq is best known for its tech stocks like Netflix and Apple.

NYSE stocks are usually identified by a two-letter unique "ticker" (stock symbol) like KO (Coca-Cola) or HD (Home Depot). Nasdaq stocks usually have four-letter tickers like AAPL (Apple) or NFLX (Netflix). Occasionally you'll also find a two-letter ticker on the NASDAQ like FB (Facebook).

Stock exchanges used to involve a lot of men standing on a floor with little pads of paper and yelling buy and sell orders. Now it's all done by computers. The computers match up buyers and sellers who want to exchange their stock for cash (or vice versa) at a specific price.

As an individual, you cannot trade directly on a stock exchange. For that you will need a "broker" or "brokerage account." A broker is simply a middleman who gives people access to a stock exchange. In the U.S., well-known brokers include Charles Schwab, Interactive Brokers, TD Ameritrade, Trade Station, Fidelity, and E*Trade.

When you are buying a stock, you will be given the choice of using two different kinds of orders. The first is called a "market order." This order tells the broker to get you into the stock as quickly as possible, regardless of price. If you use a market order, you might end up buying the stock at a price that is far away from where it last traded.

"You sell to the bid, and you buy from the ask."

The distance between the bid and the ask is called the "bid-ask spread." A liquid stock like Microsoft (MSFT) or Apple (AAPL) will have a bid-ask spread of just a penny. So right now, as I'm writing these words, there is someone at the bid for Microsoft who is willing to buy 2,200 shares for 120.25. And there is someone at the ask who is willing to sell 1,200 shares for 120.26. That's a bid-ask spread of just a penny ($0.01).

A liquid stock is defined as a stock where you can buy or sell a lot of shares without moving the stock too much. Liquid stocks in the U.S. usually have a bid-ask spread of just a penny or two.

If you place a market order to buy a liquid stock, you will usually be OK. That's because a market order will tell the broker that you want to buy your shares from the ask. Since it is just a penny away from the bid price, your order will usually be filled very close to where you are currently seeing the stock trade.

However, if you use a market order on an illiquid stock, you might get a price that is far away from the current market, or from where the stock last traded.

Let's say that stock XYZ is illiquid. There's a bid for just 300 shares at 50.00. And there's an ask for just 200 shares at 52.00. If you use a market order on a stock like this, you will have your order filled at 52.00 or higher.

If you place a market order for 400 shares on XYZ, your broker will first give you the 200 shares at 52.00. Then it will look for the next best price. In an illiquid stock, that might be another 100 shares at 52.25 and then another 100 shares at 52.50. So, you will end up getting 400 shares of XYZ at an average price of 52.1875.

Now let's say that you made a mistake and want to sell your stock immediately. If you place a market order to sell, you will first be able to sell 300 shares to the bid at 50.00. Then maybe the next highest bid is 100 shares at 49.50. If you are filled at these prices, you will end up having lost $925 (before commission), even though the stock has not moved.

That is why it is usually best to stay away from illiquid stocks. If you absolutely must trade them, you can try putting in a limit order that is right in the middle of the bid-ask spread. But there is no guarantee that your order will ever be filled.

A limit order is the second type of order, after a market order. Whereas a market order tells your broker to just get you into or out of the stock as fast as possible, a limit order specifies a price. So, if you place a limit order to buy MSFT at 120.25, your order will only be filled if there is a seller that is willing to part with the shares at that price. If there is never a seller at that price, your order will never be filled.

I almost always use limit orders in my trading, even with highly liquid stocks. So, if I want to buy a liquid stock like Microsoft, I will look where the ask is, and then just enter a limit order using that ask price. That way I won't get into trouble if a bit of market-moving news comes out one millisecond after I place my order and Microsoft suddenly spikes to 126. In this situation, if you have used a market order, there is a good chance that you will get filled at 126, even though Microsoft is a liquid stock.

When you place an order to buy or sell a stock, you will have one more choice to make:

"Do I use a Day order or a GTC order?"

A Day order will only be executed during regular market hours today. If the order has not been filled by the time the stock market closes for the day, it will be automatically cancelled by the broker.

A GTC ("good 'til cancelled") order will be good for today's market hours, as well as the following days and weeks. If you don't cancel it, it will still be working. Some brokers will automatically cancel a GTC order after a month or more, if it has not yet been filled. Check with your particular broker to find out their policies.

Standard trading hours for U.S. stock exchanges like the NYSE and Nasdaq are 9:30 am EST to 4 pm EST. Some brokers will let you trade stocks in the pre-market trading session (4 am to 9:30 am EST) or in the post-market trading session (also known as "after-hours trading" and lasting from 4 pm to 8 pm EST).

If you are going to trade before the market opens or in the after-hours market, always use a limit order.

Even normally liquid stocks can be quite illiquid (and hence volatile) during both of these trading sessions. "Volatile" means that the stock wiggles around or jumps around a lot. You may see it trading at 85, then 87, then 82, then back to 85. Stocks with lower trading volume will usually be more volatile, with a wide bid-ask spread that also bounces around.

Until you become an advanced trader, it is probably best to stick to regular market hours. And please don't ever trade an IPO using market orders. That is the ultimate newbie mistake.

Chapter 2: Creating Passive Income with Dividend Stocks

Companies want as many people as possible to buy their stock. For this reason, many offers what is called a dividend. A dividend is a payment companies issue to shareholders each quarter, which equates to a percentage of the share price. This percentage is known as the dividend yield.

For example, AT&T (T) currently sells for around $38 a share. Their dividend yield is currently set at 5.41%. This means that annually, you will earn 5.41% in profits on top of wherever the stock price moves. So, if you were to buy $10,000 worth of AT&T stock, and the price stayed at $10,000 for the entire year, you would receive $541 worth of dividends, split out each quarter. This comes out to about $135 a quarter.

Dividends are issued quarterly, when companies announce earnings. To earn this dividend, you must own a stock before it declares its ex-dividend date, which is usually about 2 weeks before the company pays out its dividend. You may be thinking why not just hold a stock for two weeks, sell it, and rake in the dividend? Unfortunately, this is all calculated into the price. What happens is on the day a dividend is paid, the stock price moves down by the same amount of the dividend payment. So ultimately you need to hold the stock for the long term to get the most benefit from dividends.

There are many companies which have increased their dividend payment every year for 25+ years straight. Knowing this, and because dividends tend to pay at a higher rate than savings accounts or government bonds, many traders of retirement age own dividend stocks. They then live off the dividend payments through their retirement years. For example, $1,000,000 is the typical amount many financial advisors suggest clients to have saved by the time they retire. If a retired individual owns a dividend stock which has a 4% dividend yield, they are receiving $40,000 a year in dividend checks. Considering most bills are paid off by retirement age (house, car, etc.), this provides plenty of income to live off of while keeping their primary capital intact. And of course, many dividend stocks rise in price over the years. This means not only are dividend checks being received, but the capital is also increasing.

Charts

There are several places to perform research on stocks, as in places where you can look at charts and financial information to see how a stock is performing. Two free websites beneficial for this are Yahoo Finance and FinViz.

There are three main charts used by various traders when viewing stocks. They include the line chart, the bar chart, and the candlestick chart. Here is an example of the stock Snapchat (SNAP) shown on a line chart.

Here is the same stock shown on an open, high, low, close (OHLC) bar chart, and then shown on a candlestick chart.

For most traders, the line chart is fine to use for everyday analysis. One disadvantage to it however is it only shows the closing price, which is displayed in the form of a line throughout the chart.

The OHLC bar chart and candlestick chart show additional information. They not only show the closing price, but also show the opening price, low, and high of a given period (5 minutes, daily, etc.). Whether a trader decides to use a line chart, bar chart, or candlestick chart is personal preference. I prefer to use candlestick charts when I am researching stocks.

And just to clarify, when you are looking at a "daily" chart, you are not looking at just one day's worth of a stock price. The whole chart shows a specified date range you set, while each candlestick in the chart shows one day's worth of trading.

If you were instead looking at a "15 minute" chart, each candlestick would be showing 15 minutes' worth of trading. A 5-minute chart, each candlestick would show 5 minutes' worth of trading, etc. The whole chart itself shows the date range you specify. If this is confusing at all, it will make more sense once you look through a few charts.

Along with the type of chart used, charts also have two scales: logarithmic and linear. The linear scale is the most common, and what is shown on almost every broker or website you visit. It displays the same amount of space between all price numbers.

For example, the chart below is a linear scale chart of AMD. You'll notice that the spacing between $10-$20 is the same as between $20-$30. However, thinking about this with a math brain, you may recognize that from $10-$20, the stock has increased 100%, while from $20-$30, the stock has only increased 50%. So, the range shown is not proportional to the percentage the stock increased, but instead just equally spaced between dollar amounts.

The logarithmic scale chart is different because it takes the percent change into account, as opposed to just the dollar range. The same stock is shown below, except this time in a logarithmic scale. As you can see, it takes into account percentage change, and spaces the dollar amounts out proportionally. Thus, it ends up showing a different looking version of the same chart.

Which scale type a trader chooses to use is a personal preference.

Volume

As briefly mentioned before, volume is synonymous with the number of trades, both buying and selling, that take place in a given period. Generally, when there is more volume, there tends to be a smaller bid/ask spread.

Volume is usually shown at the bottom of charts, in the form of lines. I have an example below with a chart of Coca-Cola (KO).

The chart shown is a "daily chart," meaning each volume bar at the bottom of the chart represents one day's worth of trading volume. So, from Dec. 2019 - Feb. 2020, between 3 million - 20 million shares of KO were bought and sold on any given day.

There are several different times frames you can look at charts, which include 5-minute, 15 minutes, daily, weekly, etc. The volume shown directly correlates to whichever time frame chart you are viewing. For example, if you were viewing a 5-minute chart, each volume bar at the bottom would include 5 minutes' worth of trading volume.

For the most part, especially if trading well-known companies, you don't have to worry too much about volume. It becomes more critical when dealing with thinly traded stocks (e.g. penny stocks), and specific trading strategies in which volume can be used as an indicator.

Stocks, ETFs, and Mutual Funds

While you're already familiar with what a stock is, you may not know what ETFs and mutual funds are. Mutual funds were the first on the block, being offered to retail investors in 1974 by Wells Fargo. Many financial advisors suggest "diversifying" a portfolio to achieve beneficial returns, while also limiting risk. This would mean instead of just putting all your money into one stock, you would split your money into multiple stocks. This way if one ends up not doing well, you have several others which will likely be okay.

Unfortunately, this was hard for everyday retail investors. Not only would you have to keep up with the top companies in the market, you would also need to pay commission on each trade. And remember, commission during this time was costly. Mutual funds alleviated all this, as they allowed investors to buy an already diversified set of stocks consolidated into one ticker symbol, which was actively managed by a mutual fund manager for a small fee.

For example, a popular mutual fund created by the company Vanguard is the Vanguard 500 Index Fund (VFINX). This mutual fund correlates to the S&P 500, meaning a consumer could buy this mutual fund with their broker, and essentially own all the S&P 500 for a one-time commission fee. The disadvantages to mutual funds are the limited hours of the day you can trade them, as well as the fees taken by the mutual fund company to balance the fund for you.

In the early 1990s, the first exchange traded fund (ETF) was introduced. Similar to mutual funds, they allowed traders to diversify their portfolio by buying just one symbol. ETFs gained more popularity than mutual funds though because they could be bought and sold like a stock during regular trading hours, and the fees associated with owning them were much lower.

Today there are hundreds of ETFs available for traders to buy, in sectors such as the S&P 500, gold, oil, retail, and any other category you can think of. Within the last 20 years, 2x and 3x leveraged ETFs have also become available, which mostly double or triple your purchasing power when you buy them.

For example, a popular ETF which correlates to the S&P 500 has the ticker SPY. If you were to buy $10,000 worth of SPY, and the S&P 500 went up 1%, your account would also go up 1% ($100). A popular 3x leveraged ETF that correlates with the S&P 500 goes by the ticker symbol UPRO. If you had instead invested this same $10,000 in UPRO, your account would be up 3% ($300).

Of course, this also works in reverse. Meaning if the S&P 500 went down 1%, your account would now be down 3%. So, the leveraged ETFs essentially become a gamble. The stock market is Wall Street's casino!

While items like contango and backwardation can affect the prices of leveraged ETFs, just know they are essentially doubling or tripling your risk/reward when you buy them. These terms are beyond the scope of this book, but you're welcome to look them up if you choose.

Earnings

Each quarter, publicly listed stocks are required to report their earnings to investors. While the exact date a company reports their earnings vary, most companies report them around the same time as each other each quarter.

Earnings are a critical metric for companies, as it lets investors know how the company is performing, and if they are making sufficient profits. Before earnings announcements, financial analysts who work in banks and other large corporations predict the earnings per share price they expect the company to announce. Generally, how it works is if a company beats estimates, the stock price will rise, while if they miss the estimates, the stock price falls. This is not always the case however, as other factors may skew the stock price.

Stocks can experience huge gains or losses on days they announce earnings, in the double-digit percentages. Generally, it's not a good idea make short term "bets" on earnings, as it's mainly playing the roulette wheel at a casino, and betting on black or red. Also, many times the analysts are wrong, and sometimes wrong big time. Don't ever rely on analysts! I would compare them to palm readers, as they do not know what is going on behind the scenes and are making "educated guesses" for their estimates.

Chapter 3: A Day Trading Strategy

All over the world, stock markets open in the morning. Those day traders who think they can start trading while munching on their breakfast, with no preparation, are among those who make losses. All businesses open in the morning. No successful business person just gets up, yawns and starts his business activities. Successful professionals arrive in their office with a clear idea of how they will tackle the work and related challenges. Likewise, to succeed in day trading, one must prepare beforehand. These preparations include many aspects; such as mental, physical, emotional, and financial.

Professional traders have clear advice for day traders; never trade if you are tired or stressed; never trade if you are feeling highly emotional, and trade with clear money management concepts. Day trading is a sophisticated business activity, where people try to earn money by using their intelligence. Therefore, physical or emotional stress can cause harm to your trading business. You will not be able to make rational decisions if you are tired or feeling stressed.

Before you start the day's trading, you should be physically, mentally and emotionally alert. A good night's sleep is necessary for traders to tackle the roller coaster ride of stock markets. Here are a few steps that will help you prepare for day trading with a cool temperament and calm mind.

Before going to sleep, keep your trading plan ready. Check the stock chart, make notes on the chart what significant patterns the price created in the previous session. Note down the critical support and resistance levels. Then mentally go over this chart and imagine how you will trade in the next session, in different trend conditions.

Do not spend too much time watching news about stock markets or anything else. Watching the news may create doubts in your mind about stock trends and influence your decision-making power for the next session. If possible, do some breathing exercises or meditation before going to sleep, which will sharpen your focusing power and reduce stress.

Also, prepare your money-plans for the next trading session. How much you will invest? What will be your loss tolerance level? And, what will be your profit booking point? During the trading hours, these decisions have to be made in a split second, and if you are already prepared, you will not hesitate to make the right decision. These will also help you set your goals for intraday trading. Just stick to your goals and you will not face any decision-making problems during the trading hours.

The final stage of your preparation will be an hour before the markets open in the morning. This is the time when you check the news reports about the business and financial world, and the economic calendar. By doing so, you will know what events could influence that day's trading pattern in the stock market. You can also check how the world markets are trading in that session. Sometimes all markets trade in one direction, which will be beneficial to know before your local stock markets open.

Planning for Trading

In day trading, financial instruments are bought and sold within the same session. Sometimes more than once through the same day. To be successful in this endeavor, traders need to know where the price might make essential moves. Technical charts are beneficial tools in deciphering this price moment. Anybody involved in stock trading relies heavily on stock charts, which is why successful traders always create their trading plans before making any trading decisions.

When you create a trading plan, you are creating an 'assistant' to help you during the trading hours. This assistant will have all the information you will need for day trading; such as trade entry, trade exit, profit booking, stop loss and significant price moments. Nobody goes looking for a treasure trove without any map. Likewise; no trader worth his or her salt will trade without a trading plan. Let us look at how a trading plan is created:

A trading plan is based on research, takes time, but saves a lot of effort and precious money during the trading hours. It is one of the most essential tools required for success in day trading. Every day trader has heard this saying 'fail to plan, and plan to fail'. Professional traders don't tire of emphasizing the importance of a trading plan. If you take their advice and prepare a trading plan before the markets open, you are halfway through to successful trading.

A trading plan is prepared before markets open and so, it is open to revisions and changes after markets start to trade and price changes. Every trader has a different trading style and based on that his trading plan could differ from others. But every trading plan must have a few essential details. These are:

1. Significant support and resistance levels: One must mark the significant support and resistance levels on the trading chart because these will symbolize the trade entry and exit points. These levels should be visible on charts to help in decision making during the chaotic trading hours.

2. Trade entry rules: Your trading plan should include when and why you will enter a trade. This could be a detailed explanation like 'if the price goes above X level, then buy'. Or it could be just a green arrow pointing to that price level.

3. Trade exit rules: Like the trade entry point, mark a trade exit or profit booking points on your trading plan. You must follow these rules meticulously, otherwise, these will become useless, if you plan and do not follow them.

4. Money management rules: Some traders like to note down on their trading plan, how much money they will invest in the next session. They keep checking their profits and losses through the session, and if the day's loss reaches its threshold; they stop trading. This is an excellent example of money discipline while trading because, in the excitement of trading, one can lose sight of what is happening with the investment capital.

These are the most basic rules to include in the trading plan. As you gain experience and get a hold of trading patterns in stock markets, you can expand your trading plans and include more trading rules in it. But always remember, these rules must be followed. A trading plan is based on research about markets, so every rule is essential. Breaking any rule will be like going against the market, which is always harmful to any trader.

Chart Reading & Candlestick Charts

Day traders use different charts for technical analysis. The main types are line charts, bar charts, and candlestick charts. Some Forex traders also use Heiken Ashi and Ranko charts, but candlestick charts remain the most favorite of traders. The reason for this popularity is its simplicity. A green candlestick shows a positive price movement, and a red candlestick signals a fall in price. Day traders use various candlestick patterns to decipher the market trend.

The candlestick charts are more than a hundred years old. These were first used by Japanese rice traders to document the rise and fall in the rice prices. It was such an accurate system that stock traders also adopted it and it has since been a famous chart creating tool.

A single candlestick has two main parts; a body and a tail or wick. The body of the candlestick shows the opening and closing levels, while the wick shows the high and low marks. A green body shows that the price opened low but closed higher. And a red body shows higher open, but lower closing in that time frame. A single candlestick can be assigned to different time frames, ranging from one second to one month. These candlesticks make various patterns on charts. Traders try to decipher the price moment by how long the wick, or the body is, and how every candlestick is placed with other nearby candlesticks.

Candlestick charts are also used for automatic or algorithm trading, where buy and sell signals are generated by various patterns formed by candlesticks.

The up and down movement in stock prices creates candlesticks on charts. Sometimes, a single candlestick can indicate a trend reversal from high to low or low to high. These are called engulfing candlesticks and are so large that they completely engulf the previous candlestick. These can be both bullish and bearish candlesticks. A bullish candlestick is formed when the price-move creates a significant positive or green candlestick, which overshadows the previous one. It signals that the price is ready to move higher and to start an uptrend.

Its opposite is a bearish engulfing candlestick pattern. Here, the stock price makes a big red candlestick overshadowing the previous one. This signals significant selling pressure and shows that the price will fall further.

Another popular form of a candlestick is "Doji". Usually, this candlestick forms near the top or the bottom, after the price has made a long moment in either direction. In a Doji candlestick, the body is tiny, and the wicks are long. A small body denotes uncertainty in buyers and sellers; which shows that the market cannot decide whether to go up or down. Such an uncertain signal on top may indicate a trend reversal, and traders prepare for a fall in the market. A Doji formation at the bottom signals that the downtrend may come to an end and traders look for confirmation of a price-rise from lower levels.

Candlesticks create many types of patterns on a technical chart. This could involve a single or two or more candlesticks. There are many books about candlesticks and how to read candlestick charts. Traders who wish to know more about these charts, can read some of those books and enhance their knowledge.

Manage Your Time Effectively

Day trading is a demanding profession and requires significant time. Any market session runs for at least 6 hours a day, and you will have to spend that much time watching and observing markets; even if not reading. Apart from trading hours, a day trader needs to research, create trading plans, and keep learning new things. All these require time and effort.

Therefore; to succeed in day trading, you will need to manage your time effectively. Usually, people want to adopt a day trading career so they will have working flexibility. This means freedom from getting up early and rushing to get caught in the morning traffic, freedom from having a boss, and of course, financial freedom. Nothing comes easy in this world. A dream life also requires putting in lots of effort. Many day traders find it challenging to complete their trading routines; such as after-hours research and planning. Part-time traders who are already busy with some other work also struggle to prepare for day trading in their spare time.

With just a few adjustments, a day trader can find enough time to complete all steps required for a successful day trading.

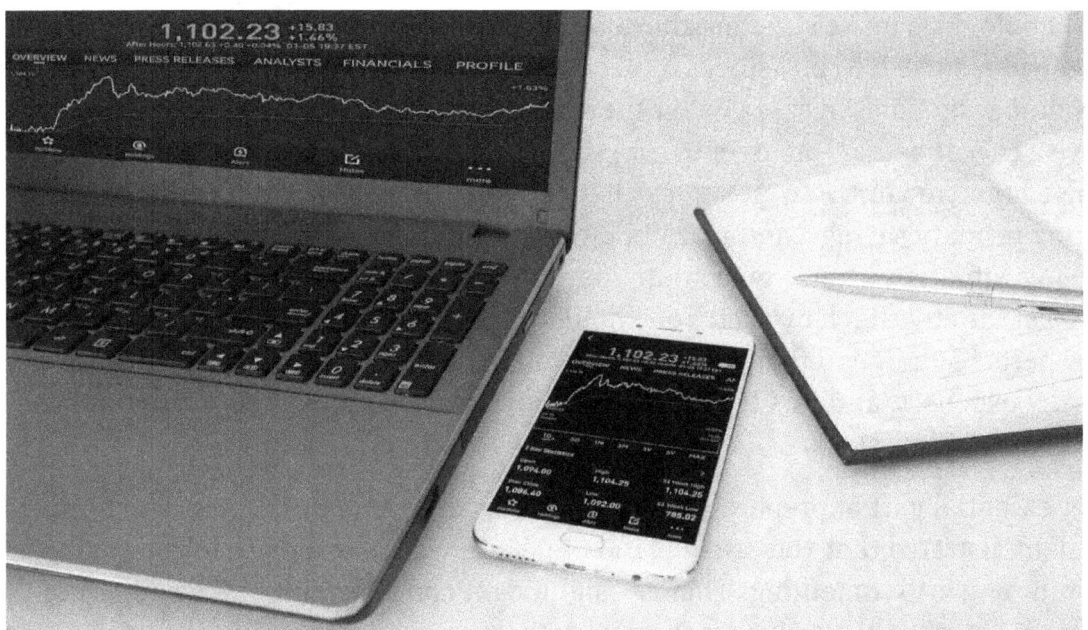

Chapter 4: Create a Timeline for Systematic Investing

Many people who decide they want to get into the stock market are anxious to do so. However, it's essential to prepare before you start buying shares. The first thing that every person should do is make sure that they have an emergency fund of cash stashed away, and that you will not use it to buy stocks or to cover losses. The purpose of an emergency fund is to have money on hand in case you hit the skids with a job or lose other sources of income if you have a car or medical emergency, or your basement floods and you need to pay for expensive home repairs. Recent surveys have shown that far too many Americans have been neglecting primary savings, and many could not even meet a $400 emergency car repair. If you are in a situation where you couldn't pay for a $400 car repair, then you are not quite ready to get into the stock market. You should work to save up a little bit of money first. Many experts recommend that you save up around six months of required funds to pay all your living expenses, and that is good advice, however that doesn't mean you have to wait that long to start investing.

Another essential part of preparation is education. And congratulations, by reading this you've demonstrated that you are the kind of person who is willing to take time to learn before jumping into something! That is a significant consideration, especially when money is involved. You should also look into courses that are available online and read as many as possible, especially when trying to determine what kind of risks you are willing to take and how to marry your investment goals with that. There are many online courses available on underlying stock investing, day trading, swing trading, options, and other topics.

In recent years the development of simulators is one of the most exciting tools for education. These can be useful, especially if you've never done self-directed investing before, but especially for those who are looking to be day traders, swing traders, or trade options. Practice makes perfect as they say, and that's as true with investing and trading as it is with anything else. If a football player needs to practice before a game, a new trader must practice day trading or options trading, before putting real money on the line.

One problem with investing and trading are that emotions ride high. It's completely natural to experience emotional highs and lows as the stock market does its usual roller coaster ride. However, what you don't want to do is let emotions start guiding your decisions and taking you over.

The process of being guided by emotion can start at the very beginning when you choose your very first stock to invest in. Ask yourself a question – why are you choosing that particular company? Are you picking different companies because you think they are cool, or because you are taking a cold hard look at company fundamentals? You should be selecting companies based on whether or not they meet your investment goals. So you should be looking at their earnings, their prospects, the P/E ratio and other important metrics that will help you decide whether or not a company is 1) in good shape both now and for the long term future as far as you can see it, and 2) that the company helps you meet your investment goals.

Maybe you are in love with Apple. But being in love with Apple is not a good enough reason to buy stock in Apple. If Apple doesn't match up with your investment goals, you should be looking elsewhere.

Emotion has a considerable influence when people are facing losses. People panic and sell off. When the Dow Jones starts declining, people start moving their cash into "safe" investments, many that these days don't even pay hardly anything like money market funds. Some people don't even do that and just sell out and take the cash.

As an investor, you need to be disciplined. The courses of action described in the last paragraph that is governed by fear and panic are not the courses of action that a disciplined investor is going to take. Now if you are a swing trader and the market is declining, then either you're going to sell, or you're going to be shorting the stock. If you are a long-time investor, however, you most certainly shouldn't follow the lemmings over the cliff. What you should be doing is looking at a downturn as a buying opportunity. So, you should be loading up on shares, but don't do it all at once. When the market enters a downturn, nobody can be sure how low it's going to go, so you want to make disciplined, periodic purchases the way you always do. Dollar cost averaging always works when you are in it for the long haul. That doesn't mean you won't miss some opportunities, but over time the market will rebound again, and by the time you are in your retirement years, the prices will be much higher than they were when you originally invested in most cases.

There are going to be some cases when you're going to want to bail. An individual stock can decline for many reasons, and sometimes there is a point of no return. For example, Bear Sterns crashed from $170 a share to $2 a share over a matter of a few weeks. If you had invested in Bear Sterns, then you should have been studying the situation closely and you would have gotten out early.

So, you might want to bail from an individual stock when the data tells you that this is the right course of action. But you never get out of any stock simply based on panic. Know what the fundamentals are of the company.

Emotion works the other way too. When it seems like a stock simply goes up and up, people can start getting giddy about it. You might be tempted to put your entire life savings into that one stock. But that is a bad idea, no matter how good the stock is. As we've mentioned before, it's great to know that Amazon increased so much that an investment of a few thousand would have made you a millionaire, but hindsight is 20/20. Right now, it's impossible to know which if any social media companies are going to actually bank profits and still be around in 20 years, so it would be foolish to put your life savings into one. The so-called investor who goes around claiming to know what the proceeding sure thing is can be called nothing more than a fool.

Another problem is people get emotionally invested in one company. Maybe it's because of the mission of the company or the products it makes that people think are going to "change the world." But when you get emotionally invested in a company, you start becoming irrational. Good examples include Tesla and Theranos. Let's take the latter case. Theranos claimed to have invented a revolutionary means to let people test their blood and to have medications delivered. It became clear that it was a sham. Still, the people who were emotionally invested in the company and the female CEO were fooled about it – and some still are even though it's clear now that Theranos is done and the CEO may even be facing charges.

In the case of Tesla, the jury is still out. They make high-quality products but have problems with delivery and scaling. They may yet overcome those problems. But if you talk to many Tesla investors, they are zealots about it. If Tesla ends up going down the drain, many of the investors may go down with it. Is it worth it?

It is important to avoid making rookie mistakes especially when it comes to money. Here are the 10 tips on avoiding the classic mistakes on stock market for a beginner.

Not Having a Regular Investing Plan

Make sure that you have a plan to invest regularly at fixed amounts. Don't worry what the amount is, you can grow it but you should have a minimum amount that you can contribute each month. Even if you are only buying one share a month right now, that is a start, you can increase the amount as your ability to contribute grows.

Not Doing Analysis

Many new investors just buy whatever stock appeals to them at the moment. At the start of your investment plan and then once a year after that, you should set up specific stocks that you are going to buy, and then stick to purchasing them at least once a month in quantities that you have decided on beforehand.

Not Diversifying enough

Many investors buy stock in a few companies and think they have a diversified portfolio. If you have fewer than 15 companies that you are investing in, then you are not maintaining a diversified portfolio.

Not Diversifying by Sector

Remember that you should not put all of your money into a single sector or industry. Take some time to find companies in different sectors besides the one you are interested in.

Panic During Downturns

Never exit the market during downturns. This is a huge mistake that millions of people make – and they do it over and over. As a long-term investor, you are not worried about downturns, which are going to be short events when compared to your entire investment history. You should invest in more stock, not less when there is a downturn, so that you can get discount prices.

Changing stocks too much

If you have found good companies to invest in, stick with them. You don't need to be continually switching around your investments and doing so will cost you in the long run.

Not Rebalancing

Make sure you rebalance your portfolio at the end of the year, so it continues to help you achieve your long-term goals.

Avoiding ETFs

Many ETFs have growth rates that outpace the market and you also get the benefit of massive diversification. You should include at least a few ETFs in your investment plans.

Sticking by a Company Too Long

While you can get out of stocks too early, you can stick by them too long as well. If it's clear that a stock isn't growing to help you achieve your wealth and income goals, don't be afraid to back out of it.

Using Money, You Can't Afford

You may not want to face it but paying off debt first is more important than investing. A debt with a 7% interest rate means you are losing 7% a year on it. So, paying it off is the same as investing in the S & P 500.

Chapter 5: Swing Trading Tactics

Swing trading is a trading strategy that uses technical information or news analysis to plan and execute one's trades. It's important to note that you can either use publicly released news information regarding a particular stock or you can use technical analysis. The key differentiating factor to swing trading is that you hang on for several days or a couple of weeks, unlike day trading, which requires you to get in and get out of the stock within the day and not a minute over.

The reason why day traders need to leave within the day is because in many cases, stocks move in price over night. They may have traded at a certain price when the market closed the previous day, but when the market opens the other day, the stock might open much higher or much lower. This is too much risk for day traders since they are often heavily leveraged. They have borrowed a tremendous amount of money to increase the magnitude of their earnings.

This also increases their risk tremendously. It's so risky that they cannot essentially park a stock overnight. It's too much risk. While it would be nice if the stock opens higher than it closed before, it's just as likely that when the stock opens, it opens below its previous close, and whatever money the day trader makes is vaporized.

The swing trader doesn't trade within a day. The swing trading strategy involves buying a stock and waiting for quite some time. This can range from two days to a couple of weeks or more. The whole point of swing trading is to make money when the stock breaks out. This is a point where the stock gets past its resistance level and keeps going up.

Usually, swing traders would target a particular appreciation rate like, let's say, 10%. Once the stock reaches that rate of return, the swing trader would liquidate his or her total position. Another way to swing trade is to liquidate your position gradually. For example, if you are sure that the stock is going to appreciate quite dramatically, then you can set up your trades so that you can sell half your holdings when the stock reaches a 10% gain.

At this point, there was a breakout that occurred. However, you keep the remaining 50% of your holdings and schedule 25% liquidation, and the stock appreciates another 5%, and so on. This way, swing traders have already locked in their gains with the first breakout.

However, since you really can't tell just how much higher a stock can breakout by using a graduated liquidation strategy, you increase the chances that you would make more money.

Put simply, you position yourself to benefit as much as possible from the breakout in trading.

Dealing with Pullbacks

It would be nice if a stock broke out and just went one direction. It would be nice if a stock broker past the certain price point and just kept rising and rising. Well, even if we're talking about Apple computers or any other historically fast rising stock, there are days where it suffers a loss. This is called the pullback, and swing traders can also make money with pullbacks.

They liquidate on a high point and then set aside a certain percentage of their capital to scoop up the stock if it dips past the certain point. Whether we're looking at breakouts or pullbacks, you're going to use the same analysis still. You're going to pay attention to the following factors to spot if a stock is either going to breakout or if it's going to pullback, how much of pullback will it suffer, and at what price point should you buy. Here are the factors that you should look at.

Bullish Trend

By looking at the volume of a stock and its price appreciation, you can tell that there is a tremendous demand for the stock, but the price hasn't responded tremendously. Pay attention to volume. This speaks quite loudly regarding investor sentiment. If you noticed that there's a lot more buying than selling, but the price seems to move very slowly, this means that there is a tremendous upward pressure.

Any small changes in the resistance to upward pressures might release the stocks from its sluggish appreciation and you may not see a nice percentage gain over several days. Look for that bullish trend. The stock must be on a definite upward swing. It doesn't have to be very pronounced, but as long as you can see the incremental rise of the stock with ever increasing volumes, then you know that something is about to blow up.

Stock Selling under Resistance

If you notice that the stock sells below the resistance level, but the resistance price seems to be stuck for a long time, this is a key indicator of a potential breakout. It seems like the people are selling, but the price doesn't drop dramatically. It remains stuck. Regardless of how much stock was sold, there's still more than enough buyer interest to keep the resistance fairly stable.

Resistance seems Stuck for a long time

This is one key indicator you should look for. If you notice that the stock is appreciating by small increments but seems to be stuck within a particular range for a very long time while volume is increasing, this is a key indicator that if some slight changes happens, there is a higher chance that the stock will spike up rather than dip down.

Increasing Trade Volume with Little Price Change

I can't repeat this enough. If you notice that there is an increased level of buying activity while the price doesn't change, pay close attention. This means that there is a tremendous buyer interest and the price seems stuck. If the selling side of the pricing equation finally slows down, expect the stock to break out. This should not be all that surprising because of the tremendous buying pressure.

Risks associated with Swing Trading

There are risks with swing trading. First of all, your money is going to be parked in stock for quite some time. This is painfully obvious if you are a day trader. As a day trader, you're normally most comfortable with quick in and out trades. Not so with swing trading. You have to content yourself with camping out on the stock for an extended period.

This can be very risky on two fronts. First of all, you could simply make the wrong bet. The stock that you thought poised for a breakout simply just sits there. This is the worst thing that can happen. If you think about it, this is worse than the stock depreciating. Why?

You're forced to wait and wait and wait. In the meantime, you're not using your capital to make money with quick gains playing other stocks. This can be very problematic. The second risk that you take is the opportunity cost because you cannot split up your trades in so many ways to diversify your risk. You need a large pool of capital to make your swing trade worthwhile. And since you're not able to do those diverse trades, you might be losing out big time.

How do you Make Money when a Stock Pulls Back and Rises?

Swing trading works both ways. You can make money from breakout swing trades. You can also make money from pullback swings. When a stock pulls back, you sell when the stock hits your target price and then you wait for any pullback. You then buy at the bottom of the pullback and then you wait until the stock swings up again, then you unload, then you keep repeating this process.

If you play your cards right, you can make a tremendous amount of money in a fairly short period. Still, that length of time can seem too long for people who normally day trade. So how can you tell if a stock is right for a pullback swing? Pay attention to the following factors. It rows previously.

The first thing that you need to look at is the fact that the stock hit a high point previously. This is important. Make sure that it has already hit a high point. It's very hard to predict a pullback when the stock is still rising. If you're in a middle of a rising stock, it's going to be hard to do a pullback strategy.

The Pullback is Recent

Now that you've found a stock that had a nice high point and then has pulled back, pay attention to how long it's been since the stock pulled back. You need to look for a recent pullback, not a pullback that happened six months ago.

You know that you're in a slow-moving stock if the pullback happened several months ago. Look for a stock that just suffered a recent pullback. Maybe less than a week, or a week, or two. It's also important to make sure that the pull back is less than 50% of the total value of the stock.

For example, if you are thinking of doing a pullback swing strategy trading on a stock that peak that $100, it's a good idea to make sure that the pullback was fairly recent and the price that you're going to buy into is not less than 50% of the $100. In this case, $50.

If the stock is trading at $30 and it just crashed from $100 peak, you might want to hold off. That stock might still have ways to fall. But if you noticed that the pullback was fairly recent but it didn't fall below 50%, then you may be able to play that stock.

Lower Volume during Sell Off than Appreciation

This is the smoking gun. If this factor is present in the trading performance of the stock you are considering for a pullback trade, you're in luck because this speaks volumes as to the investor demand for that stock. If the stock's price fell based on fairly low volume compared to how much of the stock was being bought when it was on its way up. This is a clear indicator that there's still a lot of buyer sentiment in that stock.

Pay Attention to other Strength Signals

It's important to note that when you're doing pullback swing trading, you also have to pay attention to value fundamentals. This is really important because you can't just rely on technical information like volume and incremental appreciation, or incremental declines in the prices. The reason why you're doing quite a bit of value or fundamental analysis is because you want to make sure that the stock will pull back. While you really cannot be sure if its fundamentals are quite solid, there's a higher and even chance that the stock will recover.

What factors should you look at? Well, pay attention to price per earnings ratio or PE ratio. Pay attention to the fundamental details of the company. What industry is it in? Is its industry on the upswing? Is it a market leader?

Also, pay attention to its stock performance compared to the rest of the market. If everything lines up, then the stock that suffered a recent price decline might actually be a good candidate for a pullback swing. Again, you have a window of two days to two weeks for your investment to hit its targets before you leave the stock.

Chapter 6: Forex Trading Tactics

In this chapter, we are going to discuss the strategies used by Forex traders. The discussion in this chapter is going to be of a qualitative nature. We are going to dive more into the specific tools that are used by Forex traders. Those tools involve chart analysis and technical indicators. Those are important, but it's also important to understand the overall strategies and approaches used by traders.

Everyone has their own trading style. Everyone also has their own favorites among all the tools are used in order to try and get favorable trades. As a new trader, you're going to find this a little bit overwhelming. The key for a new trader is to sample different tools and find the ones that fit their personality and abilities best. For example, if it's true that technical analysis gives certain traders an edge, but you aren't inclined to use technical analysis that really doesn't make it an edge for you. In other words, you may not be so good at using technical analysis in order to help your trades., in that case, it might be better to look for other approaches.

Candlesticks

Candlesticks and trading bars are related tools that many traders use. They both contain the same information, but candlesticks are by far the most popular. We are going to spend talking about candlesticks, but, right now, we are just going to give you an overview that discusses the information provided by candlesticks and what they're used for.

The first thing to know about candlesticks is that they tell you the open and closing price for a given trading period. By trading period, we mean different ranges of time. You could divide up your charts into one-minute intervals, or you could use four-hour intervals or even one-day intervals., if you were using four-hour intervals, that would mean that the candlestick provided the opening price at the beginning of the four-hour period and the closing price at the end of the four-hour time period. The time frame that you would use will depend on the preferences that you take when making your trades.

Candlesticks also tell you whether prices were rising or falling over the timeframe. This is usually indicated by color, with green candlesticks representing rising prices and red candlesticks indicating falling prices. Since you can either buy or sell a currency pair, the meaning and importance of the color are significant, depending on the position that you've taken. On many charts, different color schemes can be used. Normally, when colors are used to represent rising prices, are indicated with a hollow candle body. A white or black solid body would be used to represent a candlestick with the following price.

Fundamental Analysis

Many traders or investors have heard about fundamental analysis when it comes to the stock market. In that case, it means looking at the fundamentals of an individual company, such as determining whether they are positioned to continue making profits. Of course, in Forex, we don't have any individual companies. That said, there's plenty of room to do fundamental analysis. In this case, you're going to be looking at macroeconomic factors, political factors, interest rate risk and international trade. The overall health and state of the country's economy and political situation are going to have a big impact on the value of its currency.

In the present environment in the United States, for example, interest rates are far less of a factor than they have been historically. That being said, if you've been following the news, you'll realize that the Federal Reserve has been a little bit anxious to raise rates, hence, there may be interest rate increases coming. Even if interest rates are not particularly important right now, they may be important in the future. This could be in the near-term future over the next couple of years.

Scalping

Many Forex traders use a technique called scalping. This involves entering a position for a very short period of time, hoping to make profits from short-term price movements. The profit from any single trade will be small. A Forex trader that is using scalping makes up for the small profits per trade by doing lots of trades. The games that traders are looking for fall in the range of 5 pips up to about 20 pips.

The profits obtained from a single trade is actually very small. This puts the scalper in the position of having to enter lots of trades, but there are trade-offs to be made. One of the trade-offs is that scalpers tend to trade small. And what that means, is that they have low risk per trade as well.

If you have a larger account and can risk more money on a trade, then you can make tens of dollars in profit off the very small move in currency price. Putting $10,000 on the trade - depending on the kind of move you would be looking for, could possibly net you a couple of hundred dollars in profit. Since the movements they are looking for are small, they don't have to stay in their trades very long. This could make it possible to do multiple trades per day. One of the advantages would be that a trader could actually make a full time living by doing multiple trades every single day.

Swing Trading

Swing trading is a totally different approach. In this approach, the trader seeks to find big swings in market prices., let's imagine that we are hoping the price of a currency pair will rise. The swing trader will look for zones of support and resistance that define the range over which the currency pair normally trades. Then, the swing trader will wait until the currency pair price drops near the zone of support, which serves as a barrier for the lowest possible price of the currency pair. When the price moves to this point, that is the ideal entry point for the trade. When the swing trader enters a trade, they will patiently wait for the price to rise to a level over which they want to take profits. A swing trader is willing to hold their trades over an extended time. This is not a long-term trade, in the sense that they would keep their trade for a year or something like that. However, swing traders are willing to keep the position for several days, weeks and even out to a couple of months.

Position Trading

Position trading as a strategy is something that can be said to be an extension of swing trading. This is a long-term approach where you can stay in your trades for even months at a time. In this case, the trader will use fundamental analysis. That's because, over the long-term, the factors considered in fundamental analysis become more important., for example, the longer you hold a currency pair, the more important become the economic trends in the two countries. Also, there might be certain events, such as one country might raise its interest rates, so that they are higher relative to the other country. The longer that you hold a trade, the more important these types of events become.

That isn't to say that other types of analysis are not important for position traders. Position traders will use tools like candlesticks, too. That will be important to tell them when to enter a trade and when to exit a trade. Like swing traders, they will use support and resistance to help them make their decisions.

Day Trading

You've probably heard about day traders on the stock market, but there are also day traders on Forex. Day trading is basically like swing trading but using short-term time frames. A day trader attempts to get in and out of the trade during the same trading day. Trades can be held for hours, but they can also be held for short periods that last between five and 20 minutes. It's not quite scalping, because the day trader may seek to earn a much higher profit then a scalper would., like swing traders, a day trader would probably enter a trade at a level of support. Then, they would exit their trade at resistance. They also look for phenomena such as breakouts, which are sudden breaks to an upward or downward trend. Day traders are not going to be concerned about things like the fundamental analysis. You can't say that they won't be concerned at all, because there could be something like an announcement of an interest rate change that could drive the markets, but on most days, day traders are operating on a short time skill; therefore it's unlikely that such things are going to impact their trades.

Retracements

Consider a trend that is strong in one direction or another. When any financial assets are trading in the trend, you're going to see a lot of wavy lines up-and-down. In other words, the trend is not going up in a straight line and there are times when the price drops back - appearing to reverse. But then you see the price resume its inevitable climb or descent.

These kinds of moves are known as retracements. A retracement provides a trader with an opportunity to get in on the trend. The way that you take advantage of this is to wait for the price to move to a low point (if we are considering going long) and that's when you enter your trade. Then you wait for the trend to resume and take your profits at the appropriate level.

Trading a Market

One strategy that some traders use is looking for trends that occurs slightly before one market closes and another opens., for example, a trader could attempt to find a currency pair that was in a strong trend just before market close in the United States. The goal here would be to get in on the trend before it takes off as New York closes and London opens. In the financial markets, there are often strong moves which take place within the first 30 minutes when the market opens. Since Forex operates 24 hours a day, you could benefit by holding your positions after the market closes and then riding the uptrend when the next market opens.

Currency Pairs

Calling this one strategy currency pairs might seem a little facetious. Obviously, every Forex trade is a currency pair. But what we are talking about in this strategy is forgetting about focusing so much on the majors. All too many traders simply want to trade any currency against the US dollar. But that misses the point because the essence of trading - it is to get more money out of it then you started with. The members of the pair aren't really that relevant. The thing that is relevant is by how much the pairs are moving. There are software tools that you can use to help you pick out pairs that are showing strong movement in one direction or another. That way, you can get in on trades where are the big movements in price. This can help you earn larger profits. The only problem with this strategy is avoiding currency pairs that have low liquidity.

Chapter 7: Playing the Stock Market Through Mutual Funds

Mutual Funds

Shared funds pool the properties of several investors, supplying purchasing power that surpasses that of all but the wealthiest individuals.

Suppose you have $10,000 to invest. If you try to spread out the cash Around 50 stocks, commission costs alone may cripple you. Yet spend the same $10,000 in a mutual fund that holds 50 stocks, and you've got that. Buy a small piece of each of those companies without the cost or trouble of acquiring them separately.

Professional money managers decide when the fund sells and buys, and all of the financiers either win or lose together. If shared, the investment pays 10% in one year, and every person who holds the fund at the beginning of that year will see the fund—very same 10% return on his investment.

At the end of 2012, financiers worldwide had $26.8 trillion purchased Mutual funds, with $13.0 trillion of these assets in the hands of the U.S. cash supervisors, according to the Investment Company Institute (ICI). Of that, $13 trillion bought the U.S. shared funds, 45% remained in stock funds, and 26% was in bond funds.

Stock and bond mutual funds can be found in two tastes:

Passively handled funds. Frequently called index funds, quietly managed funds try to match the performance of an index.

Actively handled funds. Unlike passively managed funds, proactively handled funds purchase and offer securities to exceed the return of their standard-- generally index or index party. It's hard to overstate the value of mutual funds as a financial investment automobile. More than 92 million people own in the United States alone shared funds, frequently through retirement plans. Additionally, most 401 (k) retirement plans invest employees' possessions in pooled funds, so if you take part in a company-sponsored retirement plan, you probably currently own funds.

Pros:

Professional management. The majority of individuals do not know much about evaluating financial investments because of a lack of interest, an absence of training, or both options.

With almost 9,000 standard mutual funds on the market, practically any investor can find a fund to resolve her investment objectives.

Diversification. Portfolios containing a range of stocks or bonds tend to be less unpredictable than an individual stock or bond. Mutual-fund supervisors utilize their purchasing power to acquire numerous securities, which most of the time supply diversity.

Cons:

Every shared fund charge fees. Remember that specialist you worked with when you purchased the mutual fund? Also, some funds charge costs called loads, gathering additional money to compensate for the salesperson or investment company.

Complacency. Mutual-fund investors typically presume that considering that they have a professional handling a diversified basket of stocks, they can relax and relax. Don't make that error.

Poor returns. Last year, only about a 3rd of actively handled shared funds surpassed their criteria. A lot of academic studies recommend this pattern isn't brand-new, which fund fees should have much of the blame. While the persistent underperformance shouldn't scare you away from shared funds, it needs to hammer home the significance of choosing your money wisely.

Exchange-Traded Funds

According to the ICI, by the end of 2012, creditors had invested around $1.34 trillion in exchange-traded funds commonly called ETFs. ETF possessions correspond to barely more than 10% of the value of standard shared funds, but these types of financial investments continue to grow in appeal. ETF possessions have more than tripled considering in 2006, while the number of ETFs on the market increased to 1,239 in 2012, from 359 at the end of 2006.

ETFs operate much like mutual funds because they blend the resources of many financiers to acquire a basket of stocks, bonds, or both. ETFs vary from traditional shared funds in a couple of important ways:

Switch on platforms. As the name suggests, these securities are traded on almost the same markets as stocks. ETF rates change from second to second, just like stock prices.

Mostly index funds. While a couple of ETF managers actively handle their funds in an attempt to top standards, the bulk of them tracks indexes.

Greater openness. Unlike traditional mutual funds-- which the SEC requires to divulge their holdings quarterly-- ETFs need to disclose daily. Considering that indexes don't change their holdings typically, a lot of ETFs don't either.

Pros:

Convenient trading. Unlike the way shared funds reprice at the end of the day and trade only at that cost during the following day, ETF costs rise and fall intraday like stocks.

Hedging. Financiers can purchase and sell options on ETFs, just as they can on the majority of Inventory. Starting buyers will probably avoid stocks, but the flexibility to buy and make choices. ETFs permit has contributed to their popularity.

Trading costs. Numerous brokers charge more to trade mutual funds than stocks. When investors buy or offer exchange-traded shared funds, they pay the same commissions charged for stock trades.

Cons:

Fund costs. Bear in mind that every shared fund charge fees. Since ETFs trade like stocks, investors often treat them like stocks and forget about those charges. And ETFs rarely draw much attention to the fees they gather.

Selection. Many ETFs track indexes, indicating they're passively managed. While some ETFs use active managers, financiers looking for active management will discover a couple of choices amongst ETFs.

Viewed complexity. While ETFs appear like mutual funds in the majority of aspects, many investors avoid them. A 2010 survey by Mintel Compere Media, a consulting firm, found that almost 60 per cent of financiers decided not to buy ETFs because they did not understand how they operated.

Certificates of Deposit

Standard Deposit Certificates (CDs) serve as enhanced savings accounts. Investors lend money to a bank that then consents to pay a fixed interest rate — usually for a term of 5 years or less.

Whereas creditors can withdraw cash from a savings account at any time, CDs need to keep the funds at the bank until the date of maturity. These tend to pay higher interest than traditional cost-savings plans because of this limitation.

CDs can't change any of the other financial investments pointed out. They supply you with a way to produce more interest on your money holdings than you'd obtain from a bank cost savings account or a brokerage account.

Pros:

Security: Like other bank accounts, CDs are guaranteed for up to $250,000 by the Federal Deposit Insurance Corporation (FDIC) in the event the bank stops working. Brokerage accounts do not receive FDIC protection, though the Securities Investor Protection Corporation (SIPC) does provide similar, if less extensive, defense.

No fluctuation. Since your funds remain in cash, they won't decrease in worth.

Simplicity. If you understand cost savings accounts, you already understand much about how the CDs are running.

Cons:

Low is returning: Although CDs usually deliver more interest than bank savings accounts, they will pull all the other investment groups mentioned over the long term.

No liquidity: CDs tie up your money for some time. You can access the cash if you need it, but you'll pay an early withdrawal penalty or forfeit some of the interest.

Separate accounts: A lot of investors buy stocks, bonds, and shared funds from institutions other than banks. If you keep your money in a bank CD, you must keep it at the bank, which indicates you can't redeploy it to buy stocks or bonds up until you move the money to a brokerage account.

Alternative Assets

For the most part, new investors must stay away from anything other than the securities gone over in the preceding pages. When you dip your toe into the market, you may hear about different investment options, including the following:

Nearly 100 commodities trade on markets worldwide. Financiers can gain commodity exposure by acquiring stock in a business that deals with those products or they can invest straight via a futures contract. Futures contracts allow investors to purchase or offer products and other assets for predetermined rates in the future.

These derivatives enable stock or ETF financiers to bet on whether shares will rise or fall without purchasing Shares themselves. Suppose the stock trades are worth $50 per share. If the stock is $55, you can either buy the stock at a discount rate or sell the call option at a profit.

Hedge funds. These entities pool financier money like shared funds do, but they tend to pursue unusual or esoteric methods. Hedge funds, gently managed and often deceptive, frequently handle massive threats.

Precious metals: Investors purchase valuable metals as a hedge against inflation, or as a backstop to safeguard wealth versus a disaster, assuming that when catastrophe wrecks the monetary markets, metals such as gold will retain their value.

Antiques: While financiers can generate income in antiques, a lot of lack the marketplace competence to profit regularly.

Of course, plenty of financiers value the inflation protection and total-return potential of real estate and would like to purchase in. Since some estate cost so much, a couple of people have the funds to invest straight in the property beyond their personal houses. These companies purchase, offer, and handle real estate, and their trust units' trade on exchanges like stocks.

Weighing the Options

No matter how completely you examine the choices for prospective investment, how much caution you take in crunching the numbers, how much time you take to research the stock exchange and the forces that impact it, you're going to make errors. A great deal of them.

Extreme boasting about returns and success rates is among the best methods a newbie can find the posers. Boasters end up being especially aggressive during bull markets-- when lots of stocks are hitting brand-new highs. If you're listening to the wrong voice, you're going to end up high, dry, and perhaps ashamed when the market corrects.

Before you buy into some pundit's sure-fire strategy, do some of your own work.

Stocks

Common stocks supply financiers with an ownership interest in a company. Shares of stock represent business equity and are called equities. Financiers can purchase and offer stocks on exchanges entities that exist mainly to produce a market for the shares. Stocks trade continuously during business hours- 9:30 a.m. to 4.00 p.m. Eastern time most weekdays with prices changing from 2nd to second.

As the value of business fluctuates, so does the cost of an investor's stock. Over the long haul, stock rates tend to rise when companies increase their earnings and sales. However, in the short-term, stocks can gyrate, moved by things like total financial patterns, news from rival companies, government action, and other aspects.

At the end of August 2013, Microsoft shares sold for $33.40, with about 8.44 billion shares outstanding. If you increase the number of shares by the per-share cost, you get $282 billion, the stock's market capitalization, frequently abbreviated to market cap. A financier who acquires 50 shares of Microsoft for approximately $1,670 would own a small portion of one of the world's largest companies. When more people wish to purchase a particular stock than to offer it, prices tend to increase. As any economics book will tell you, when items end up being scarce and the demand for them increases, prices often increase in reaction.

Chapter 8: Make sure you have the Right Tools to Trade Profitably

In this chapter, we will be looking at the tools you can use in order to make sound investment decisions. To make sound decisions, you need to base them on solid fundamentals. That is why the tools presented in this chapter are financial models which can help you evaluate the performance of a company. Upon proper evaluation, you can determine if the stock is right for you, or you can take a pass on it until its fundamentals improve. These models are based on quantitative analysis. Much like technical analysis, quantitative analysis refers to basing decisions on the number and measurable data. While your instincts are definitely important, it is data-driven analytics that will give you the peace of mind that you need when making an investment decision. At the end of the day, you can be confident that you made the right call based on the analytics which you have used to base your investment decisions.

So, let's jump right in!

Tool #1: The Three-Statement Model

This model lives up to its name.

It is based on the analysis of a company's financial statements. Hence, the name "three statement model" refers exactly to this type of model.

To conduct the right analysis, you will need to have the following financial statements: balance sheet, profit and loss, and cash flow statement.

In this model, what you are doing is essentially linking all three statements so that they make sense of the company's financial situation. You can use this model to get an accurate idea of a company's overall financial position. If the numbers show health financials, then you can feel that the company is in good shape and will produce good results down the road.

Now, the way this model works is that you will find a way to link all three statements into one model. What you can do is take the trend of each statement and look at the way they all move together. So, if all three statements show a trend for growth, then you can be sure that the company is in good shape.

However, if one the balance sheet is growing, but the profit and loss and the cash flow show signs of trending in the opposite direction, you would need to figure out why this is happening. There could be some unexpected situations, but the company is still solid.

If the company is posting profits, but their balance sheet is taking a hit, then you can assume that their financials are out of whack. In this case, you would really have to evaluate if this investment is really worth it. Perhaps it might, but a very short-term deal.

The use of this model is perfect for value investing and identifying the potential for a turnaround in a company that's been under water in recent history.

Tool #2: Initial Public Offering Model

An initial public offering (IPO) is the even in which a company switches from being a private company to be a publicly traded company. In this event, the company is valued at a certain price per share by that company's financial team, and then the IPO is underwritten by the bank, or investment firm, that is essentially sponsoring the IPO.

The issue here is determining the right IPO. This is based on the company's book value, and then a comparative analysis is conducted on the IPOs of other similar companies to see where your valuation can fit in.

When you conduct your comparative analysis, you need to consider a set of variables which can be compared among companies. For example, you can compare revenue, gross sales, number of employees, annual turnover, growth rate, and so on.

The actual variables which will be considered can all be compared in a large spreadsheet.

Then, each variable can be contrasted with the comparably-sized companies so that you can visualize if the results obtained correspond to the comparable.

If you find that your company is above the variables seen in most comparable, then you might be able to value your company at a higher per share price. If you see that it is below, then you might want to reconsider going public at that time. You might want to hold off going public at that time and wait until the company's financials improve.

Now, as an investor, the IPO valuation model is very useful since it allows you to see how individual companies stack against each other. This allows you to determine if your choice to invest in an IPO will make sense for you, or if you're better off waiting for the stock to prove itself in the market first.

However, I would like to recommend that you consider getting into IPOs whenever you have the chance since being one of the early stockholders can provide you with an opportunity to clean up when the stock takes off. As such, investors who get into the early stages of an IPO can position themselves for making good gains. This can happen when you understand the comparable of that company's IPO. You can see if the valuation makes sense, or if it's being valued too high. In which, you might want to wait to see what happens in the market first. If you see that the valuation is below comparable, then you might be looking at a potential bargain.

Tool #3: The Revenue Model

This model consists in charting a company's revenue over a given period to see the trends in that company's revenue.

You can build a model for each company you are interested in trading based on its revenue.

The best way to build this model is to take its historical revenue reports, chart them and then calculate its trend line. You can do this on commercially available software such as Microsoft Excel, although your brokerage firm may offer you this type of analytics so you won't have to calculate it yourself.

So, how can you interpret this model?

Once you have charted the historical data for a company's revenue, you can then look at its trend and determine if it is growing or declining. I would recommend that you look at 10 years' worth of data since it will give you an accurate picture of where the company is going. This would be 10 years of quarterly reports. That means that you could have 40 different data points where you can contrast the company's trend.

With this model, you can see if the company is still expanding, leveling off, or declining.

When you see that a company's revenue is growing, you might consider it to be in an expansion phase. Depending on the age of the company, it could still be developing as part of its growth phase. If the company has been in the market for a longer period of time, say at least 50 years, you may want to take a look at older data, for example 25 years, and see if the company is having a renaissance due to factors such as management turnover, the introduction of new products, or a shift in market conditions.

This model is simple since it only looks the behavioral patterns of one variable over time, but it is the most powerful variable in stock trading. You can then overlay a company's revenue trend line with that of other economic variables such as Gross Domestic Product (GDP), inflation, consumer confidence, and major stock indices to see if the company is responding to the factors around it, or it is producing results in spite of the trends observed in the overall economy.

The best part of this model is that you can overlay as many variables as you like to get a sense of where that company's revenue is going as compared to any number of variables in its surroundings.

Tool #4: The Forecasting Model

Industry experts will produce forecasts for companies' revenue.

These forecasts respond to the available data that analysts are looking at when determining where a company's earnings report should fall. These forecasts will produce an actual Dollar figure which estimates where that company's earnings report should fall.

Usually, forecasting is done on an earnings per share basis. This means that the per earnings per share price are calculated based on that company's track record and other variables which can be taken into account such as economic conditions affecting it, and any other variables which may come into play.

From that, analysts will produce a forecast where they expect that company's earnings per share to fall in line.

This is where analysts' expectations are bred. If the company beats analysts' expectations,

Tool #5: Resistance Level Model

This model takes the trend in moving averages to determine where "resistance" levels can be found. A found resistance level is a psychological barrier that investors and traders must pass in order to continue with the stocks trend.

Resistance levels are seen both at the top and the bottom, that is, both the floor and the ceiling of a stock.

If a stock is trending upward, you may often see that it won't pass a certain point. This would be a resistance level. And, it is often hard for a stock to break through a resistance level because investors may not feel comfortable with paying a certain price above a previous high.

In order to determine resistance levels, you need to look at the candlesticks of a stock and then compare it to its overall trend at the different points for moving averages. It could be that the 10-day moving average is trading in a given range, but it is not surpassing the high point of the 200-day moving average.

When you are in the presence of a resistance level, you can choose to approach the stock in a number of ways.

First, you can choose to day trade the stock within that range. For instance, you can set up a buy order when the price falls to the lowest point you have observed in its 10-day or 50-day trend. Then, you can set up your sell order when it hits the resistance level ceiling.

This strategy can help you make some decent if underwhelming profits. But as long as the stock doesn't break the resistance level, you can feel confident about trading within that range.

Tool #6: The Gap Up Model

When stocks close on high at the end of a trading day, investors may be looking to continue pushing the stock upward at the opening of the next trading day. This is common when a company's report data in the afternoon of a trading day. Since they may report data at 2 o'clock pm, for example, that may not provide investors enough time to make the most of the stock's positive results.

As such, investors may choose to wait until the next trading day to pursue this stock. As a savvy day trader, you can purchase the stock right at the beginning of the trading day and wait for the gap to fill. When you hear that a "gap is filling," it means that the stock will go back to its previous highs after the euphoria has passed.

Chapter 9: Opening your Trading Account

The application process is very simple. The brokerage company will have you fill out a few forms to open the account, execute a (separate) margin agreement, and you will add an options agreement to your account (only if you wish to trade options). These applications will gather information on you to make sure you are credit worthy and that you have the experience and understanding to trade your account at the various levels they may approve.

Experienced investors often qualify for all levels when they open the account, whether they intend to trade them initially or not; this keeps you from having to do more paperwork later, when you do wish to trade them.

Beginners don't need the margin or options agreements. For more experienced investors: If you only want to buy CALLS and PUTS, and sell covered CALLS, a margin agreement is not required. If you want to place debit and credit spreads, you'll need to have the margin account. To trade more advanced strategies, the brokerage company needs to know you have the experience and financial resources to trade these higher levels.

You should read the technical brochure carefully – Characteristics and Risks of Standardized Options and make sure you understand the risky aspects of this type trading. You shouldn't have any problem understanding this brochure and the options agreement once you have read this.

It is, by law, the brokers responsibility to gather this information on your financial resources and trading experience; most use a group of standardized questions on the applications.

Understand which of these levels are suitable for you before you apply for the account so you can communicate clearly with your trading company.

The Functions of Your Online Broker

Tech support: It is quite normal if you are new to your broker - that you will have some questions on how to install and operate the software, a.k.a. "The trading platform." There are scores of training videos, articles, webinars, and written instructions either on line / in a manual to help you learn to operate the software. It is imperative that you open a practice session (paper trading account) so you can familiarize yourself with all operating aspects of the software and to learn about the services your broker offers. Some of the brokers have 'for fee' services; my advice it that until you gain a lot of experience, you do not sign up for any of those. You will find more than enough to explore and learn without buying additional services. You should try and find answers to your questions by viewing videos and reading instructions as much as you can. When you get stuck, phone your broker and they will get you going again. As a courtesy, it is the custom that you should be as quick and specific as you can when you phone them for help. Brokers usually have a text chat help service also.

Real-Time Quotes Bid/Ask Prices: One of the first things you'll do with your new online account is to build watch lists. You simply put in symbols of stocks you wish to follow and the software will give you the bid/ask prices, change for the day, the ability to pull up charts for each stock, ETF, or Index, and more.

Charting-Trading Tools: When you view charts, the horizontal axis will be time/dates and the vertical will display the prices. Begin using bar charts, which display the high, low for various (selected by you) intervals of time, like 1m, 5m, 15m, 30m, 1h, 4h, 1d, 1w (minute, hour, day, week.) If you wish, you may learn more about technical indicators and charting in your software. There are a hundred or more indicators, but four or five of them are used most commonly: MACD, Bollinger Bands, Resistance-Support, Momentum, and so on. Your broker will have professionally made videos you can view free – on just about any subject.

Statements and Trade Confirmations: Your daily transaction summary, statements, and confirmation notifications are listed in the program and usually you will receive daily email notifications of your transactions. When you enter an order, you will get a 'fill' the moment a transaction occurs – and usually a sounder to alert you also. The 'fill' is the same as a confirmation and gives you time/date stamp, transactions, prices, and other information. Paper statements are normally sent at the end of each month, but you can get your account status and balance, and a record of your transactions anytime online.

Entering Trades, Buying and Selling: Follow the instructions to enter trades, you will enter the quantity, price, and the type of order you prefer to use. All trading software will allow you to enter an order, and then to check it again before you SEND it; this is to avoid mistakes.

Investment Tracking: There is a section in your trading platform that will always summarize your trades, current valuation of them, and list them in an easy to interpret format. This section is sometimes called position summary or another similar term.

Research Educational Material: Every online broker provides customers with many tools that include charts, news items, research material, and more to help you find the information you need. Anytime you need help, you can ask your broker to suggest videos so you can train to use the software's many valuable features. It will be time well spent. You can use your smartphone or other device to watch this material on your own convenient schedule. Also, most brokers provide chat rooms where customers can talk among themselves, and this is a way to find ideas and help.

Money Transfers IN & OUT: When you open your account, you may mail a check if you wish. Most commonly, monies are transferred in/out of your account by wire transfers (or an equivalent) directly from your bank. You can call account services of your broker and they can help you set this up and answer your questions. Be aware, some banks and/or brokers charge varying rates for these services. Ask your broker for suggestions, if you need help in finding the best way for your particular needs. Often, banks have ridiculous fees to make these transfers, so be sure and ask 'how much' before you authorize the transfer.

Choosing a Broker

Online brokers typically charge from $4.95 to $12.95 per transaction (regardless of the number of shares you are trading of a stock.) To be clear: Whether you buy one share or a thousand shares, each transaction will be charged this flat fee. There is one transaction for each security (stock); you can't combine stocks into one order. Often brokers will offer a number of free trades to new accounts, so ask about that when you call.

While brokers who charge $9.95 for a trade are charging almost double the $4.95 rate, it is better to use a broker that has good software, technical service, and is a good fit for you – rather than trying to save a few dollars on stock commissions. You might save $5, but wind up with software you don't particularly like; this is not advisable. In the long run a few dollars more in commissions here and there should not be a deal-breaker if you get the broker you like. Where you might pay $9.95 for a trade, you are still getting a good deal since full-service fees easily range from $25 and up.

Here's a partial list of some brokers you may wish to consider; go to their web sites and take a look at their trading platform (most will provide you samples or at least a video).

Often brokers will have more than one version of software. For example: a simple version for just buying and selling stocks; this version uses the simplest of screen interfaces and is very easy to use. Secondly, most experienced traders will opt for the version (still absolutely free) that has more features.

The Importance of the Trade Simulation Mode

Sometimes, starting off with the more complicated trading software can be off-putting to beginners and they opt for the simpler version until they gain some confidence. Remember that your broker will have a trade simulation mode where you can learn to use the software without having to use real money. Your mistakes there won't cost you anything; this is a valuable service to learn to use the software, so go for it, explore and learn. This can be quite fun to trade paper money until you get the hang of things.

The experience of using a broker's software can vary widely, so you might wish to compare two or three before you decide. The brokers understand this; they help new customers every day. Ask questions, and see how user friendly your new broker will be!

The importance of learning to use the convenience and power of the trading software furnished to you by your broker cannot be overemphasized. Not too long ago, trading 'paper money' accounts, merely kept a list of trades and P/L (profit/loss). Now, you must learn to think of your trading software as your control center of trading and research. Being able to use your software is key to your success; it has powerful features and it will serve you well to spend the time to learn to use it. Your broker has free videos to make learning easy. Viewing several short videos works much better than watching hour-long videos – and this avoids information overload. As you are trading it is important to have confidence in your ability to find and use information. Use the trade simulation mode of your broker like a pilot would use a flight simulator. Think of it as a valuable and accurate trading tool and hone your skills with it so you can remain focused on your trading and not have half your attention diluted by not learning to use your software seamlessly. It's actually quite fun to trade in 'paper money' mode. It's a great way to test some ideas and gain confidence and experience without any of the risks.

Chapter 10: Choosing a Stock and What You Need for Trading

Finally! The moment you've been waiting for: time to buy your first stock. Now that you have an account set up with the broker you chose, you need to tell them what to do. Sit down with your plan and take a look at the mix of stock types you've decided will make up your portfolio. Now we'll begin to look for stocks to fill them. Here are the things you should look for in each and every company you're considering investing in.

What to Look For

These factors work together to determine the overall value and promise of a company. All or most of these need to be strong to make buying a share of ownership in the company a good idea. These factors together will give you an overall picture of the health of the company now and a clear window into its likely health in the future.

Revenue

This is usually the first thing on the income statement. Revenue is how much money a company is bringing in the door, not accounting for expenses or any other adjustment. When looking at revenue, what you're hoping to see is a steady increase over a decent period of time. Within the same year, quarterly reports may fluctuate wildly depending on the type of company, but you want to see a year-to-year incline in revenue overall.

P/E

This abbreviation stands for Price-Earnings Ratio. A lot of experts consider this the single most important number to look at when considering purchasing a stock. While that is debatable, it is certainly very important. The P/E is a single number representing the result of some simple math. First, the company's overall earnings are divided by the number of shares outstanding, giving the Share Earnings. Then, the price of the stock on the market is divided by that number. Here's an example:

Company X earned $500,000 last year and has 10,000 shares outstanding. This means its share earnings are $50. If the stock is selling for $200 per share, the P/E of this stock is 4.

Whether you're looking for a low or higher P/E is based on the amount of risk vs reward you're looking to assume with the purchase. If a stock is a good value, its P/E should be low compared to other companies in the same industry.

Net Earnings

This is the revenue minus all of the expenses the company incurs. It's easy to think that a higher net earnings line always means the company is in a better position than one with a lower net earnings, but this isn't necessarily true. Some reasons a company might show a low net earnings but still be strong are restructuring, major innovation or product development, and changes in management. These could improve the earnings for the upcoming years greatly.

ROE

Return on Equity is the measure of how well the company is using the money that it makes to improve share value. It is calculated by dividing the net income for the full year by the shareholder's equity (the total of all assets minus the total of all liabilities. Note: preferred stock should also be subtracted as a liability. It is not part of common equity.) This number should again be low relative to other companies in the same industry.

Debt Ratios

This is the ratio of all debt to all assets. You'll usually see it notated as a percentage or decimal. A high percentage doesn't always mean the company isn't being managed well. As with ROE, look at several years averaged together and at other companies within the same industry.

Future Earnings

Obviously, we don't have a crystal ball, but we can get an idea of how a company will probably do in the near future. Companies publish "forecast future earnings." Be aware, though: these are the opinions from within the company and tend to be overly optimistic. In order to glean a picture closer to reality, look at forecasts from the past and compare them to the actual performance, and that will give you an idea of how far from the mark the reports tend to be.

Competition

In all of these measures, you've been comparing each value to the same value of other companies in the industry. While you have that in front of you, take a closer look at the competition. If they have new products that look promising and innovative, that could make the stock you're looking at less attractive.

Where to Find Information

When a company goes public, allowing its shares to be traded on stock exchanges, it has to file reports on its earnings and the state of its financial health in order to stay in good standing with the Security Exchange Commission. This is great news for us because a lot of the information we need to buy with confidence is contained in those forms. There are three commonly published forms, the 10-K, the 10-Q and the 8K. These all contain different information for different periods of time, but looking at all or some of them will give you an insight into the following aspects of the company.

The 10-K is released once a year and contains the fiscal information for that year. It is audited by an outside accounting firm.

A 10-Q contains some of the same information, but covers only a 90-day period of time and isn't usually independently audited

An 8-K is not released on a set schedule, but whenever major changes are going on within the company. Good things like acquisitions or deals the company has made are included, as well as bad news like SEC investigations. Any material event that could affect the shareholders is an inducement for the release of an 8-K, and it isn't unusual for several to be filed throughout the year. Honestly, these forms do not make for the most exciting reading.

Stock Screeners

This is a ton of information to look at for each stock you want to buy, but there's really no way to be a smart investor without doing it. Luckily, software specifically made to filter through the mountain of data available can help. Stock Screeners allow you to set the parameters of stocks you're looking for, such as relative risk, debt ratios, stock type, and a lot of the other determining factors. Then, it only shows you the relevant information for stocks that fit those parameters. This can be an invaluable time saver, especially when first building your portfolio.

Analysts

Television and the internet are full of opinions on investing. While some of these sources are invaluable, a lot of them are better at getting attention than providing useful advice. Finding analysts whose opinions you respect and whose values align with your own may not be easy, but it will be worth it because you'll have something to check your gut instincts against.

You will see all through this guide about what you can do to learn the securities exchange. To make it work, you should prepare the correct assets for exchanging purposes. There are several things that you will need that are designed to help you keep tabs on the market while also being able to keep performing well.

Enough Money for Trades

To start, you will need to establish a sensible budget for day-trading. You should determine the amount of money you are willing to spend on your trades. More importantly, you have to think about what you are willing to lose. There is always the chance that all your trades could be duds. You should plan your budget based on the assumption that you will not actually make a profit. Playing the stock market is about finding ways to make money without spending too much in the process. You will require a minimum capital of $25,000 to trade on the market. This is enough money to help you exercise many trades without requiring leverage or margins. You could still use leverage or margins in some trades, although that is a completely optional solution.

The United States Securities and Exchange Commission or SEC states that you need to have $25,000 or more in equity if you plan on trading:

1. Anyone who day-trades four or five times within five business days will need $25,000 or more in equity. The SEC interprets day-trading as a practice where you buy and sell something on the same day.

2. You must have this amount of money ready if the day-trades in your portfolio total at least 6 percent of your overall trading activity during the same five business days.

If you can, add more than the $25,000 required into your day-trading account. A bit of extra money gives you a buffer to work with.

Sensible Strategies

Create a strategy that you can use for your trades. Your strategy may be based on factors like:

- How you will enter into a trade

- How you will get out of that trade
- The total risk you have in each trade
- An analysis of how well a stock is performing

As you will discover throughout this guide, your plans for doing well in stock market investing should include multiple strategies in your trading plans based on what you discover based on your research and general common sense.

Online Resources

You will need to use quality online resources to help you manage your trades. There are various trading platforms that will assist you in identifying what stocks are available, will help you to execute trades and ones that list all the details about how a stock is moving. Historic information should be provided to you through one of these resources. A stock screener is also vital to your investing success. This helps you have information on stocks based on specific criteria. You just add individual parameters into the program and it would then find choices that fit.

A Proper Education

Although you are not required to hold a degree to trade on the market, you must at least have the proper training. It is best to take advantage of an online program that teaches you about what is available and how to make trades. Of course, if you are reading this guide then the odds are you already understand the many points relating to online trades. There are various online trading schools that could give you information about how the market works. Groups like the Online Trading Academy, Trade-Pro Academy, the Stock Whisper, the Day-Trading Academy, Winner's Edge Trading, and many other groups have their own online programs.

A Strong Mindset

The most important thing you need for day-trading is a good mindset. You need to be mentally prepared to trade and ready to accept what might occur and be prepared to respond immediately when something unexpected happens. Whether it is the price suddenly dipping or an option coming at the right time, you have to know when to play the market and when to stay out of it. You must also have a mindset that focuses on a strategy and staying with it throughout the entire investment process.

Chapter 11: How to Buy and Sell Stocks

Now that you have understood the basic parameters to look for in a good stock, you are ready to move to the next step, buying the stock you like. This process isn't difficult once you have your brokerage account.

E-Trade, TD Ameritrade, and Merril Edge are some of the online brokers you can choose for buying stocks online.

Buying a Stock

You must pick the stock only after doing thorough research. Look at the fundamentals of the company thoroughly. In the beginning, you may not understand all the technical jargon given in the 'financials' segment.

There is a big difference in buying stocks with a long-term perspective and buying them for intraday trading. Intraday traders are more focused on the daily movement of the stock prices. As a long-term investor, you don't need to bother about the daily movement of the stock. Even if the price of the stock has fallen in the past few days, but the fundamentals of the company are strong, and there is no negative news about the stock, then you can buy it.

This is a decision you must take, depending on your ability to invest. As a beginner, you must not invest all your money in one stock all at once no matter how bright the stock may appear.

First of all, make a careful decision about the amount you want to invest in. If you have $100 to invest, don't put all of it in the first trade. Buy a few shares and then observe the stock performance for a few days. This will give you greater confidence, and you will be able to invest more in that stock later with more optimism.

Investing all your money in a single stock is not a good idea as you would lose the chance of diversification. You may feel that it is a small amount, and you can take the risk of losing that money in a stock. However, that is again a short-term perspective.

If you want to invest for the reason of wealth creation, you would be investing more money at regular intervals, and this will increase your stake over the period of time. Investing smaller sums into several stocks will wider your reach and you would be more open to considering other stocks too. It will prevent your money from getting locked in one stock in particular. It is a habit that you will have to build. Many people think that they'll invest in other stocks when they have more money but end up investing all they have again and again in one stock itself as they haven't expanded their search area. Any specific negative news can then affect their investment adversely in their case.

Order Type

When you are ready to buy the stock, you will come across several technical terms on the trading platform that you will need to understand.

Ask Price: This is the price that the seller is looking for at that moment. This is not the final price on which you have to buy that stock. You can wait for that price to come down a bit due to market fluctuation, and you can also put your own price somewhat lower than the asking price. This is just the price the seller is ready to accept for the sale of that stock at that moment.

Bid: This is the price you can set for buying a stock. You will have to enter this price when you bid for the stock. If you want to buy that stock, it is generally prudent to keep it near the asking price, or the trade may not get executed.

Spread: This is the difference between the highest ask price and bid price at that moment.

Limit Order and Market Order: These are important terms that you need to understand.

Market Order: When you buy stocks at the market order, you are actually expressing your consent of buying the desired number of shares at the current price of the market. If you are going to buy a limited number of shares, then the trades would get executed immediately at the current ask price. However, if someone is trying to buy a very large number of shares at market order, then the actual price at which the trades get exacted may be higher as the trade can take longer to execute and the seller may increase their asking price looking at high demand. Remember that the stock market functions of demand and supply mechanism. The higher the demand the greater would be the price.

For long-term small investors, market orders are the best as they ensure that your trades get fully executed at the same time. If you place a market order in 'after hours' or after the trading has closed for the day, your trades will get executed at the beginning of the next working day. In that case, there can be a variation in the price.

Limit Order: Limit orders are good for intraday traders who are buying stocks for smaller margin profits. To them, even smaller trade margins matter and hence they use this feature. However, limit orders have no guarantee of getting executed as they will only get executed when they hit the fixed price mentioned by you. Generally, this difference is very small and that's why it wouldn't matter much in the long-term.

Selling a Stock

Selling a stock at the correct time is also equally important. The whole point of keeping a close watch of your selected stocks is to remain fully aware of their performance in the market. It is a fact that in the long-term, the companies with strong fundamentals usually perform well. The reason is very simple; the companies are inclined to grow. There is a complete system that is trying to make a profit and as a result, even your money invested in that stock makes a profit.

However, this may not be the case for every business venture. There can be times when a company that has been doing everything right starts to move on a downward curve. There can be many reasons for the downfall of the company.

First – The Value Judgment

Here, it is very important that your decision to exit a stock must not be a knee-jerk reaction. You must understand that many people try to square off their positions in a fundamentally sound company at the first news of anything bad about the company. Many a time there is nothing substantial about such gossip and the companies come out of the initial shock reaction very fast. But, if you try to exit a stock when many other investors are also trying to do the same, you will be looking at a major loss. Remember, the market works on a demand and supply rule. When most people are thinking of selling their stocks, and only a few people are ready to buy the prices of the stock would go down rapidly.

But, in the case, you have a strong reason to believe that there is something wrong with the fundamentals of the company or something is happening which might damage the prospects of the company in the long-run, it would be wise to make an early exit before the market gets panic-stricken. Your decision should not be emotional but financial in nature.

Second- The Order Judgement

The next thing to do is to judge the type of order you want to place. Like buying, you can place the orders too as a market order and limit order.

Market Order: In case you suspect there is something very wrong with the company, and there is a chance that panic like situation may arise, it is good to make an early exit. Through market order, you will be able to square off all your positions in that stock at the market rate and wouldn't have to wait for long.

If you have placed your order in the 'after hours,' the order will get executed at the start of the next business day at the prevailing rates.

You will have no control over the rates in such a situation, and whatever the rate at the time of opening will be your orders will get executed at that price.

Limit Order: You can place this type of order if you don't feel that there is anything wrong with the company but want to book your profits for some other reason. The limit order option gives you better control over the price you'll get.

The required details would be:

Quantity: The number of shares you want to sell. Here, you can choose to square off your complete position or rebalance your stock position a little by selling off a few stocks in this firm. Fill in the exact number of shares you want to sell.

Order Type: In this section, you will have to fill the kind of order you would like this to be. This means you want to place a market order or a limit order.

Time in Force or Order Expiration: The next thing that you would have to put will be the 'time in force' or order expiration. This clearly states the period of time for which your order would be valid.

This is a feature put in place to give you better control.

The various terms you may come across in it are:

Day: This means your specific order can be good for the day, and you might want to have a different price or strategy for the next day. If you place this order and the trade doesn't get executed the same day, you will have to place a big again on the next market opening.

Good till Cancelled: You can also place an order that's good for as long as it takes to execute that order or before you cancel it. This gives you freedom from placing the bid again and again for that stock.

Immediate or Cancel: You can also place an order under this category to dump your holdings in that stock immediately. However, any part of the order that remains unfulfilled will automatically stand canceled, and you will have to place a bid on it again and if you want to square it off.

Fill or Kill: This type of order is placed if you want to square off a large position all at once. You can place an order, and this will only get executed if your complete position in that stock is getting squared off.

On the Open: This type of order will get executed at the opening of the market. You will not have any specific control over the price on which it gets filled. It will be highly dependent on the sentiment about that stock price at the market opening.

On the Close: This type of order will get settled at the price prevailing at the time of the market close.

Chapter 12: The Hidden Evils

Many people become fixated on the price when they get involved in the stock market. They want to get in, so they look for the best prices and fail to really pay attention to anything else. The reality is, the successful involvement of investments and the stock market means that you are capable of identifying the value in things as well. An important rule of thumb is that the price is what you pay and the value is what you receive from your payment.

Understanding the difference between price and value is important because it can be the difference between investing in a stock that is going nowhere, or investing in a stock that is going actually to earn you some money. When you invest in stocks without understanding the value of what they are genuinely worth, then you may end up investing in something that holds little to no value at all. The price may be inflated, but it is unlikely that it will actually stay that way. Once the value of the product or stock itself is revealed, the company value will go down and therefore so will the stock value. However, if you invest in a company knowing that their value is high and will likely increase, then you can feel confident that the value of your stock will increase, too. When this is the case, you can almost certainly guarantee that the sale price of your stock shares will increase over time as well.

Becoming a billionaire investor means that you have to understand the difference between price and value. A good rule of thumb is to consider the value separately from the price itself. If you were to evaluate the company, or if you read professional valuations, what do they look like in comparison to the price on the market? If the price is lower than the valuation, you are likely looking at making a good investment that will earn you a great deal of money over time. If, however, the valuation is on par with the price, or lower than the price, then you know that the price merely reflects an inflated market and does not mean that you will get your money back over time.

When people enter the stock market, they often fail to pay attention to value altogether. They look at prices alone. They see a stock available at a low price and automatically assume that the value will rise, without ever taking the time to find out if it actually will or not. When people get caught up in the price and fail to look at anything else, they are almost guaranteed to fail entirely when it comes to investments. They will likely find themselves investing in things that are not increasing in price adequately, and therefore they either fail to make money back, or they lose money.

If you want to become a billionaire investor, you have to be able to make adequate decisions that will lead to you making money. Investing in the stock market is no different from investing in a business itself: if you wouldn't trust the business to give back your $100,000 investment, why would you trust the stock price to rise? A business that has a strong valuation that is believed to increase over time is one much more worthy of investment than one that may or may not increase in value over time. Just because the stock market heavily focuses on numbers and price values does not mean that you should only focus on the number.

Warren Buffett believes that if you want to become wealthy, you must learn to decipher the difference between price and value and take both into account. If you want to make the most money, you should always invest in a company that is selling shares at a low price with a valuation that is higher. This reduces your risk and almost guarantees your likelihood of getting your money back, plus profits.

"Cash is to a business as oxygen is to an individual: never thought about when it is present, the only thing in mind when it is absent." This is a famous quote recited by Warren Buffett, emphasizing the importance of cash and why people must pay attention to their cash value and be forward thinkers.

Buffett believes that we must pay attention to the importance of cash even when we do have it so that we do not find ourselves in a position where it is absent, and it is all we can think about. His company, Berkshire Hathaway, has successfully survived many recessions and market crashes because of one primary thing: Buffett is adamant about keeping an "emergency fund" and maintains one for his company. He understands the importance of this fund and refuses to let anything happen to it.

In 2008 North America faced one of the harshest recessions of our time. Many report that almost a decade later we are still recovering from it. Many companies went under at that time, falling to the deadly grips of the recession. Berkshire Hathaway, however, was not one of those companies. While many investors were rapidly selling off stocks for below cost and losing thousands of dollars, Buffett's company was busy buying them up. The company was able to use their emergency fund to remain above water, while also making many lucrative deals to buy excellent stocks that ended up making the company a phenomenal amount of money when the market started to come back up.

Buffett is so keen on keeping this fund that he insists that his company maintains a minimum of $20 billion in the emergency fund at all times. At the time of writing this, he had $85 billion in it. Although you likely will not need as much in your own emergency fund, it is important that you consider this fund and the importance of it. This fund needs to be comprised of cash. It should not be an "emergency credit card" or "emergency line of credit." While these are valuable, they are not ideal. What you need is an emergency cash fund that is an asset for you, not a debt. Having this fund means that if anything ever goes out of your favor, you are still covered. It means that you are not one bad paycheck away from filing bankruptcy, rather that you can handle these rainy days and come out the other side safe and sound.

As an individual, your own cash should have enough money to cover you during a hard time. Consider having enough money put away to cover you for a few months if you were out of a job, enough money to pay off outstanding debts, and enough money to make wise investments even if you do not have active cash flow. You want to have enough money that you can continue to live your life comfortably and still make power moves with your finances, even if your cash flow slows down or stops for a period of time.

Having this amount of money not only means that you have savings for a rainy day, but also means that you will experience significantly less stress in your life overall. While this may not seem like much, beyond a clean bill of mental health, it actually does a great deal for your ability to make investments. When we are overly emotional or stressed out, we are more likely to make errors in judgment and take actions with our investments that could be detrimental to our success. Investors who become billionaires are those who are able to handle their emotions well, and who do not allow them to come in the way of their investments. When you are not stressed that you could be in the deep with just one wrong move, then you are free to make decisions without fear. You are not worried about losing money because you know that you are safe either way and therefore you are able to put more trust into yourself and your judgments. You are less likely to pull the plug on a wise move out of fear of losing everything. You are also less likely to invest money into something that may show promise to help you "get rich quick," and actually result in you losing everything.

Being able to understand the value of cash and having an emergency fund on hand is vital. There is a reason why Buffett insists his company has one, and it is the same reason why his multi-billion-dollar company continues to thrive, no matter how many recessions or market crashes are experienced. Unlike many other stock market-based companies, his thrives in all conditions because he has built his company to be sturdy and durable regardless of the current market conditions. You should do the same not only with your investments and your business but with your life. Knowing that you are safe and prepared no matter what happens can help you have the freedom to make the decisions you need and want to have success in your life and investments overall.

Chapter 13: Masters Insight

Benjamin Graham

One of the underpinnings of Benjamin Graham's financial counsel to speculators is that, at a specific value, ninety-nine out of one hundred organizations in presence become appealing at a specific cost. This is genuine notwithstanding for the organizations that you distinguish as average, basically on the grounds they could hypothetically arrive at a cost so low you can't resist the urge to do okay.

Take an organization I could never need to claim over the long haul: Best Buy. Under a Graham examination, there is where the organization gets so modest it would fundamentally turn into a fruitful investment over the mediating years. We should stipulate that the speculators in the commercial center in some way or another choose to value the offers at $10 each. That would thump the valuation down from the current $14 billion down to $3.5 billion.

In the interim, the organization is as yet siphoning out $850 million in yearly profits. It's hard not to get rich when you purchase a stock with a 24% income yield. Best Buy could basically pay out the majority of its profits as earnings, you'd have your investment come back to you inside four years essentially because of the money extricated from the venture.

That is an extraordinary model, however it's the manner by which Graham's investigation works: you size up each organization, and figure at what costs things would get so modest that you really wanted to profit. Not very many stocks will exchange at those "gimme costs," yet when they are, you ought to hold onto the chance and purchase.

Philip Graham
Try not to Get Anchored to a Price

For the little financial specialist needing to purchase just a couple of hundred portions of a stock, the standard is exceptionally straightforward. If the stock appears the correct one and the cost appears to be sensibly alluring at current levels, purchase at-the-advertise.

The additional eighth, or quarter, or half point that might be paid is irrelevant contrasted with the profit that will be remembered fondly if the stock isn't acquired. Should the stock not have this kind of long-run potential, I accept the financial specialist ought not have chosen to get it in any case.

Here, there is a proviso for financial specialists who execute huge lumps of offers. For their situation the demonstration of purchasing/selling huge pieces at market cost may itself cause the cost to vary a great deal. So, remember that this heuristic of "purchasing at-the-showcase value" bodes well for small speculators managing moderately modest number of offers.

Try not to Buy Based on the "Tone" of Annual Report

Numerous multiple times, the yearly report content (with the exception of the financials) is composed by an advertising organization rather than the administration themselves. Also, it is difficult to make sense of that. The administration has a personal stake in showing an excessively hopeful image of the organization. Fisher cautions –

It is well to recollect that yearly reports these days are commonly intended to develop stockholder positive attitude. It is critical to go past them to the basic certainties. Like some other deal's apparatus, they are inclined to put a company's "best foot forward." They only here and there present adjusted and complete discourses of the genuine issue and troubles of the business. Frequently they are excessively hopeful.

Warren Buffet

Buffett's decision subsidizes, the Vanguard 500 Index Fund Admiral Shares, returned 7.1 percent exacerbated every year, while the bin of mutual funds his rival picked redeposited a normal of just 2.2 percent, the Wall Street Journal reports.

Buffett and Protégé Partners initially put about $320,000 each into bonds that would acknowledge to $1 million throughout their bet, but since the bonds acknowledged a lot quicker than anticipated, they chose to purchase 11,200 Berkshire B shares, which are presently worth $2.22 million, as indicated by the Journal.

How Warren Buffett makes long haul investments

Also, as chose in the first wager, the cash will go to philanthropy. Buffett's pick: Girls Inc., an association that supports young people in Omaha through after-school and summer programs.

Despite the fact that there are no assurances in the stock market, Buffett's conviction that record funds are a savvy investment is strong advice that nearly anybody can pursue.

File funds are a type of aloof investing. They hold each stock in a list, for example, the S&P 500, including enormous name organizations, for example, Apple, Microsoft and Google, and offer low turnover rates, so charges and expenses will in general be low too.

Buffett explicitly prescribes them as an approach to help retirement investment funds. "Reliably purchase a S&P 500 minimal effort list support," he told CNBC's On the Money. "I believe the thing bodes well for all intents and purposes constantly."

Peter Lynch

1. "The run of the mill enormous winner...generally takes three to ten years to play out."

Really extraordinary riches are made over years and decades. In that capacity, financial specialists ought to be set up to hold their stocks for extensive stretches of time so as to augment their additions.

2. "Around here, in case you're great, you're correct multiple times out of ten. You're never going to be correct every time out of ten."

You don't need to be immaculate to do well as a financial specialist. Some portion of the magnificence of stocks is their topsy-turvy hazard profile. While a stock could lose 100% of its value, as well as can be expected ascent 1,000% or progressively after some time. So, a couple of huge victors can more than compensate for your washouts.

3. "What the stock cost does today, tomorrow, or one week from now is just a diversion."

For a long-haul financial specialist, unpredictability and hazard are two altogether different things. A stock's everyday developments are unessential. Financial specialists would be ideally serviced by endeavoring to diminish hazard - characterized as a changeless loss of capital - over their investment time skylines. In such manner, a quicker center around quarterly - and, stunningly better, yearly - working and financial outcomes would be of more noteworthy use than a superficial take a gander at regularly deceptive day by day features.

4. "The genuine key to making cash in stocks isn't to get frightened out of them."

The greatest test to clutching your stocks is dread. Alarming features and dread mongering savants can cause even fervent bulls to scrutinize their perspectives. That is the reason it's so essential to know why you possess your stocks. That way, as Lynch says, you can "remain by your stocks as long as the major story of the organization hasn't changed."

5. "In case you're fortunate enough to have been remunerated in life to the extent that I have, there comes a time when you need to choose whether to turn into a captive to your total assets by giving an incredible remainder to expanding it or to let what you've aggregated start to serve you."

William O'Neil

Do an online quest for incredible financial specialists or extraordinary investing books, and you're certain to see William J. O'Neil's name appear in the main 10 records. He has a phenomenal investing record dependent on his very own arrangement contriving called CAN SLIM and established the warning administration Investor's Business Daily. In the wake of beginning in the investment business in 1958, he began his very own financier business in 1963 and Investor's Business Daily in 1984.

His book, "How to Make Money in Stocks: A Winning System in Good Times and Bad," was first distributed in 1988 and has since racked up four versions, the latest of which was distributed in 2009 (the release that is used here).

O'Neil's investing style is more diverse than those of most advocates of value investing or development investing. He has a foot in the two camps, he holds onto specialized just as crucial examination, however, is generally known as a development financial specialist.

Support up these declarations was his very own exploration; at its center are diagrams of the best stocks in every year for the past 125 years (this book was distributed in 2009). His models (not really set at one year) include:

C: Current quarterly income and deals (the higher, the better).

An: Annual income builds (watch for noteworthy development).

N: New items, new administration, new highs (purchase at the ideal time).

S: Supply and request (shares exceptional in addition to huge volume request).

L: Leader or slow poke (which is your stock?).

I: Institutional sponsorship (pursue the pioneers).

M: Market course (how you can figure out how to decide it).

O'Neil said of his recipe, "It's put together 100% with respect to reasonable verifiable investigations of how the stock market has really functioned as opposed to on our genuine belief or anybody else's, including Wall Street's ... or on the other hand scholastic scholars. Moreover, human instinct at work in the market basically doesn't change."

Bill Miller

Here Miller makes a point that helps me to remember George Soros' (Trades, Portfolio) hypothesis of reflexivity, which he clarified in a 2009 exposition in the Financial Times:

"I can express the center thought in two generally straightforward recommendations. One is that in circumstances that have thinking members, the members' perspective on the world is constantly fractional and twisted. That is the rule of unsteadiness. The other is that these misshaped perspectives can impact the circumstance to which they relate on the grounds that bogus perspectives lead to wrong activities.

Chapter 14: Advance Stock Market Strategies and Tactics

Short Selling

Short selling is the sale of a stock that is not owned by the seller. You may borrow the stock from some other investor or a broker.

Short selling is based on the perception that the price of a stock would decline in the near future. You can buy the same stock which you have short at a higher price, at a lower price later. You would be able to make a good profit by short selling if things occur as you thought.

You may do short selling for speculation. You may also do short selling for hedging the downside risk of your long position in a stock.

However, it is better for you to avoid short selling until you've acquired more experience in stock trading. This is simple logic because a short sale has a theoretically infinite risk of loss due to the fact that a stock may rise to any price level.

For example, you believe that the stock XYZ, which is trading at $20, will decline in price. You borrow 50 stocks and sell them. You are now "short" 50 stocks of XYZ as you sold a stock that you did not own. Your short sale was made possible through borrowing the stocks from another investor or your brokerage.

After 10 days, the price of XYZ falls to $10 due to poor quarterly results. You can now buy the 50 stocks, give them back to the owner, and make a profit of $500. You may have to pay commissions or interest on the margin account out of your profit of $500.

But if the price of XYZ rises to $40, you will incur a loss of $1000.

You have to take care of the two metrics while short selling. Short interest is the total number of stocks sold short as a percentage of the total outstanding stocks of a company. Short interest ratio (SIR) is the total number of stocks sold short divided by the average daily trading volume of the stock.

You also face a risk of buy-in. The brokerage, you borrowed stock from, may close out your short position at any time if it feels that the stock is hard to borrow or the lenders want it back.

Short selling is often disparaged for its speculative nature; however, it has some good aspects as well. Short selling gives liquidity to the stock markets. It also prevents stocks from rising to very high price levels on hype. Short selling may be a good tool for risk management.

Buying on Margin

Buying on margin is purchasing stocks by paying the margin i.e., a part of the total purchase price of the stocks. You can borrow the balance from your broker.

You need to make an initial payment to the broker for buying the stocks on margin. You need to give the collateral for your borrowed funds, and the stocks in your account with the broker serve as the marginal securities. You'll need to open a margin account with a broker who provides the facility to buy on margin to get started.

You need to fund at least 50% of the purchase price of a stock with cash. You can borrow the remaining from your broker.

Your broker sets an initial margin, and you fund the initial margin in your account before you can begin buying on margin. You need to keep some maintenance margins as well in your account.

The maintenance margin denotes the minimum amount of funds you must keep in your account. If your funds in the account fall below the maintenance margin, your broker may force you to deposit more money.

Buying on margin gives you some benefits. You can buy more stocks by leveraging borrowed money from others. You can amplify your gains when the value of your purchased stocks increases.

Buying on margin has a lot of risks as well. When you buy on margin and the value of your stocks fall, you would need more money to fund the margin requirements of your account with the broker. If you are not able to fund the margin, then your broker may close out your position. Thus, you may have to bear more losses due to the sudden selling of the stocks in a falling market. So, your losses are magnified when the price of your stocks decline in value.

A margin call occurs when the funds in your brokerage account fall below the maintenance margin. Your broker calls you and demands that you bring the balance in the account back to the required maintenance margin level. You can do this by depositing additional cash into your brokerage account or, you can sell some of the stocks that you purchased with the borrowed money.

For example, you buy 1000 stocks of company ABC at $10 per stock. You deposit $5000 and borrow $5000 from your broker. After 2 years, the stock price doubles to $20. You sell stocks for $20,000 and pay back your broker the $5000. You triple your money and make $15000 on a $5000 investment. This is leveraging someone else's assets.

If the price of the stock falls to $5, you sell the stocks for $5000. You pay this back to your broker. Thus, you lose all your money owing to buying on margin.

Day Trading

Day trading refers to the buying and selling of stocks within the same day. As a day trader, you may engage in buying and selling of stocks multiple times during the course of a single day.

Day trading aims to take benefit of the small movements in the price of the stocks. It is always hectic and stressful whether you're making profits or incurring losses.

Day trading is a dangerous style of stock trading, particularly for those who are new to the game or for those who are overwhelmed by emotions and don't stick to a well thought out strategy.

Day traders make money from minute price movements in individual stocks. They often leverage vast amounts of funds to exploit price differences.

Day Trading Parameters

You need to take care of the three parameters: liquidity, volatility, and trading volume.

Liquidity indicates the ease of doing a transaction in the stocks. High liquidity facilitates your trades.

Volatility is a measure of the anticipated daily price range of a stock. High volatility means large profit or loss.

Trading volume indicates the total number of trades for a particular stock in a day. A large daily volume is an indication of a high level of interest in a particular stock.

Scalping is a popular day trading strategy. You sell almost immediately after your trade becomes profitable. The price target is a price which is higher than your purchase price plus any transaction cost.

Momentum is another popular day trading strategy. You trade based on some news releases or events related to the stock. You buy on the news releases indicating some positives for the stock and then ride the trend until it shows signs of reversal.

Day Trading Tips

- Acquire knowledge of proper trading procedures, the latest news of events that affect stocks, stock market trends, etc.
- Fix an amount for day trading, i.e., usually 1-2% of your total investment funds
- Start on a small scale with trades involving a small amount of money.
- Avoid penny stocks.
- Start with the middle hours of a trading day, which are less volatile usually.
- Use Limit Orders for controlling losses.
- Control your emotions during trading hours.
- Chalk out an elaborate plan or well-defined strategy and follow the same with discipline.

Day trading is a challenging skill and requires a lot of time, effort, and discipline. Most of the people who try it fail and some fail miserably. You should always follow one rule: Set and strictly follow a maximum loss limit for a trading day, which you can afford without financial distress.

Online Trading

Online trading is buying and selling stocks through an internet-based trading platform. The online trading platforms are usually proprietary and generally belong to the brokerages. It is also known as e-trading.

Online trading has increased by leaps and bounds since the early 2000s, especially with the introduction of powerful computers and high-speed internet connections. Nowadays, many investors use online trading platforms for investing on their own.

You can have many facilities on online trading platforms. You get multiple tools for trading and investing. You can place, buy, and sell orders for various stocks. You can place multiple types of orders, like market order, limit order, stop-loss, etc.

You can check the status of your order in real-time. You can also view the real-time quotes for various stocks. Some of the online trading platforms give you an excellent dashboard with various facilities and tools for tracking your investment portfolio, checking transaction history, etc.

Many brokerages that have an affiliation with the banks provide you the added convenience by linking your bank account with your investment account. This allows you to do transfers between your accounts easily.

Online trading has dramatically reduced the costs of trading. Most of the brokers have also lowered the commission for trading online.

Online trading with lower fees has helped many people get started in stock investing. The brokers have ramped up their online trading platforms with automated trading. This way, they save much money that would have been spent on human resources.

You can benefit from online trading in terms of the high speed of execution of transactions since no paperwork is needed.

Before opening an online trading account with a broker, you should check the broker's past track record, tools, and facilities offered, etc.

You should also be aware that all types of stocks are not available for online trading. For example, you may not be able to trade a stock online, that is trading on the pink sheets or over-the-counter market. If you want to place an order for such a stock, you need to call your broker and hand over the task.

Portfolio Management

Portfolio management is the process of investing in various types of financial instruments such as stocks, bonds, mutual funds, fixed deposits, etc. to create a diversified basket for meeting your investment objectives.

It emphasizes on the selection of the right type of stocks which meets your risk-return objectives and give you the optimum returns on your investments.

The fundamental principle of portfolio management is the minimum risk and maximum return, keeping in view your investment requirements and constraints.

Asset allocation is the key element of portfolio management. Asset allocation is based on the long-term mix of assets. Different types of financial assets are not the same - some are volatile; others are stable. Asset allocation helps in optimizing the risk-return profile through investments in different assets with a low correlation between them.

If you want an aggressive profile, you can invest more in stocks. If you want a conservative profile, you can invest more in stable assets like bonds.

Portfolio management may have the following objectives based on your expectations and requirements:

- Capital Appreciation
- Consistent Returns
- Preservation of Principal Amount Invested
- Marketability of Stocks
- Liquidity
- Risk Diversification
- Tax Planning

Chapter 15: Brokers and Platform of Trading

As the trading markets are quite volatile in nature today, finding out the perfect broker for your trades might turn out to be a tough job for you if you are willing to generate a good amount of profits. This chapter is all about a range of tools that have been included right after extensive research. All the platforms that you will find in this chapter can provide you with all those tools that are necessary for making trades. Every platform of trading is unique in its very own way. Getting all the knowledge before opting for a platform of trading prior to making trades is very important. So, in this chapter, you will be finding a comprehensive list of all the suitable platforms for trading of options.

E*TRADE

All those traders who are completely new to the market of trading will need some help in order to understand the way the trading derivatives can help them in order to improve the returns of their portfolio. E*TRADE comes along with a very advanced form of a platform that has been designed with elegance and is capable of guiding you all throughout your way. As you get acquainted with the options and derivatives, the platform website, in addition to the mobile application, can provide you with all the help that you need for learning. This trading platform allows the users to place all the frequently used tools right in front of them so that there is no need for digging in here and there for finding then out when needed. The platform of E*TRADE also provides the users with a wide collection of resources using which you can develop the senses that are required for trading of options. All the tradable form of assets can be accessed right from the mobile application.

This platform also comes along with the function of paper trading that will allow you to test all your strategies on the platform right before you decide to give them all the capital. A very special type of tool named as Spectral Analysis is also provided by Power E*Trade. This very tool can help you to assess the maximum amount of profit or loss that you might make for one particular strategy that is used by you. You will also be able to gain knowledge about the several types of risk metrics and also the various ways in which they can affect your trade. While talking about options trading, E*TRADE does not incur any form of fees per leg. For most of the clients, the commission of per-contract is $0.65. All those traders who can place more than 30 trades in a single quarter, for each contract, the commission will be $0.50. If the price of the contract is equal to or even less than $0.10, all the fees are waived off.

Tasty works

If you have the wish of being a trader who uses options frequently, Tasty works would be the perfect choice for you. This platform comes along with a wide range of useful tools that are concerned about liquidity, volatility, and probability. According to the information that has been gathered from the platform, most of the trades that are made using this platform are derivatives in nature. So, the entire team of this platform is more dedicated to the designing of a wide variety of tools that can assist you with all the required help. Opening up your account on this platform is a very easy task. Right after you have created up your account, you need to download this platform. One of the best things about this platform is that you can play all around the platform before you start investing all your capital.

The primary concept that is available in this platform is watchlists that you can access very easily from the left-hand side of your device. The watchlists that you will find on this platform are the same on web and mobile applications both. You will also find the latest trading videos on this platform. Weekly videos are released, and you can also watch the pre-recorded videos.

Ally Invest

Ally Invest comes along with a very low brokerage cost. The best thing about this platform is that you will not need to maintain any form of minimum balance in your account. The platform is supported by Ally Financial. The users can get a universal form of experience related to the management of their accounts. The website of the platform is super easy to use. This platform of trading might turn out to be a great choice for you, specifically if you are completely new to the world of options trading. This is mainly because the platform provides users with excellent customer service. The platform is very user friendly, and in order to learn to trade, you can start with a very small amount of investment. Also, you will not need to get tensed about any form of trading fees. You will have all the time that you will need in order to learn trading as the overall risk factor that is involved is quite low.

While placing your orders on this platform, you can do it even with your eyes closed. You can also modify all your settings, view the necessary charts, and also go for technical form analysis just like a breeze of wind. You will get 36 drawing tools along with this platform. The platform of Ally Invest has been designed in a very clean way that makes it properly readable and can also be understood very easily.

TD Ameritrade

If you have just started with trading of options, the platform of TD Ameritrade would be a great choice for you. This platform of trading is also trusted by some of the well-known traders of options who are recognized for their expertise in the market. The main thing that makes this trading platform a superb choice for the trading of options is the excellent collection of resources for all the beginners, low percentage of commission, and also the reasonable form of pricing. No matter if you are a novice in options trading or an expert, this platform comes along with something for everyone. The commissioning system of TD Ameritrade was changed in the year 2019. It was initially priced at $6.95 for every trade along with an extra $0.75 for all the related contracts. At that time, the pricing was actually too huge when compared with all other brokers.

For options trading, TD Ameritrade charges $0.65 for each contract, and that can be considered as a common rate for all the platforms of trading. This platform offers users a charting feature that is very much advanced in nature when compared to the other platforms. You will have the power to check real-time data analysis with some clicks only. The trading tools that you will get with this platform are impressive as well. In simple terms, the only possible limit for the tool list of this platform is the sky. You will be able to do anything you want in this platform, starting from analysis of all your earnings to the revisiting of all the historical data of the markets. You can also measure volatility by using the earning analysis tool.

Robinhood

If you are looking out for a cheap trading platform, Robinhood might turn out to be a good choice for you. Although some of the traders are not satisfied how all the trades in this platform are being handled, it is still a great platform for all those users who are a novice in the trading of options as it comes with less risk. As this platform comes with zero fees for trading, you can easily sell or buy options without any kind of risk more than the initial investment from your side. This platform is based on the web, and it lacks behind when it comes to the aspect of providing tools for research and education. You can get stock trades that are free from any form of commission, ETFs, a certain number of cryptocurrencies, and also some finite number of ADRs. This platform can provide you with real-time notifications for all the trades and investments that you make on the platform.

Trade Station

This platform started off as a software company for the traders and was later changed into a platform of trading. If you are willing to have high-speed execution of trade along with professional-class data on a platform that is par to the level of experts, Trade Station is the perfect choice for your use. This platform charges $5 for each trade with an additional $0.50 cents for each contract. It also offers the traders with the pricing of per-contract. If you are a professional in the market of trading and want to make high-volume trades, you can enjoy the flat rate of $1 for each contract in place of paying the per-contract fee + the base fee that is being charged by a majority of the platforms. While this platform does provide much for the new and beginner traders, you can easily host a business portfolio on the platform with no problem at all. The tools provided by this platform are excellent in nature. All that you need to do is to maintain a minimum balance of $2,000 or at least five trades in a year for avoiding an annual account charge of $95.

Charles Schwab

This platform is well-known for excellent customer service. Right after you have opened your account, the cost of trades will be $0.95 along with $0.65 cents for each contract. For the first time, clients can enjoy 500 trades without any kind of commission for the first two years as you deposit $100,000 or even more in your account. Charles Schwab offers users with average kind of education and research offerings. Also, you will be able to use the platform on the web, mobile, or desktop. It is one of the best platforms for trading of options for beginners. With the availability of large content of research, you can easily get into the world of high-speed trading with all your senses open for opportunities and risks. You will need to maintain a minimum account balance of $ 1,000 to enjoy all the benefits of this platform.

Lightspeed

Lightspeed is primarily focused on the experienced and active type of traders. The platform charges $0 for each trade along with $0.60 cents for each contract with a minimum of $1 per trade. The tiered form of pricing starts from 500+ contracts every month. Relying on your volume of trade, the discounted rate ranges from $0.20 cents at a total of 100,000 contracts every month to $0.50 cents at a total of 1000 to 2000 contracts every month. This platform is all about the expert traders that deal with professional kind of trading. The platform offers an integrated form of analysis, execution of orders, analysis of historical market data, customized nature of layouts, and several other features that are of great use for the traders of options. You can easily maintain your account from the web, desktop, or right from the mobile application of the platform. This platform is not at all friendly for beginner traders.

Chapter 16: Facts and Numbers to Help You

This area is where we are delving deeper into the fun world of stock market fundamental analysis. This would consist of looking at company numbers and figuring them out to see if they make the cut for us to monitor them. The big question is always how do we do that?

The Value Question

This is always one of the first things you will encounter when you come up to anyone who is looking at the stock market through the lenses of a fundamentalist. Does this company represent value and is the value already realized by the stock market?

Some folks live and breathe the idea that you can solely rely on fundamentals to invest in the stock market. They are not wrong. I have seen and been in touch with people who have never seen a stock chart in their lives, and yet they have gone on to make millions investing in the stock market. One of the more common denominators to these people are the following:

- They start out with more than normal quantities of resources as compared to the average joe on the street.

- As a result, they tend to have a better grip on their trading psychology on the average

- They tend to make their money on occasions when the markets have drastic movements, which means they are definitely not day traders or short-term investors.

- Occasions that come to mind are like the 2000 tech bubble burst, as well as the 2008 mortgage notes crisis or the Lehman crisis.

- They do not need to depend on the earnings from their investments for their day to day living and expenses.

Fundamentals could be all you need to get ahead in the game of investing in the stock market. You use fundamentals to pick a good stock, and then steadfastly wait for either the stock price to be depressed such that it becomes a no brainer for you to buy the stock, then sell it when the overall market becomes overly buoyant, to cash in on the greed of others.

This would mean loads of patience, because you would then need to wait for that afore said event, which would bring the stock price below the value that you know it has. Usually the no brainers would be systemic events, where the overall stock market is affected and all counters take the hit. This is because when the fear is so widespread, it affects all counters without really accounting for much logic or thought. This also means that the prices getting depressed have a higher probability of just being affected by sentiment rather than having any real structural issues within the company. If the event were just centered on the specific company, then more brain work would be needed to sieve through the facts and noise in order to determine if the value which you previously saw in the company still exists.

Investing via fundamentals is really a game of waiting, where you wait to get in, and then you wait further to get out. To be honest, it is not cut out for all folks. I mean, if we look at a simple situation of a normal middle-class family, where both adults are out to work and you know they have some excess cash every month which they place in the bank account. For these folks who may have built up a small nest egg of say $50000, to get them to plunk it all down during a period of depression, when stock prices are mostly low, would be easy to say on paper, but harder to do without any form of practice.

These folks probably would be better off having constant exposure and learning as well as understanding more about their investing and trading psyche, which will then place them in a much better stead during big opportunities presented in times of financial turmoil.

Think too about the person who wishes to day trade, because he may have a sizeable sum to start off with, but because of his decision to rely on that sum to generate his monthly income, this method of fundamental investing may not be quick enough to sustain a reasonable lifestyle.

So, my view stands that fundamental investing is all good and is perfectly able to stand on its own two feet. It is just like bringing a sword to a battlefield. It is a worthy weapon to have. And now I pose this question to you. Why bring one sword, when you can actually wield two?

My personal take on this is as what I have mentioned earlier in the other segments. I use fundamental analysis for the purposes of filtration because that is the innate strength of looking at fundamentals. You get to see, as far as numbers and annual reports are concerned, the strength and competencies of a company. This ensures that I will only restrict my trading and investing shortlist to companies which have good and proper standing. I mean, if we are interested in Starbucks, we probably can summarize their business as selling coffee, and that is how we would shape our thinking and look at other facets of their business model.

Having the sword of fundamental analysis with you gives you the ability to pick and choose amongst the huge pool of stock candidates out there, and that would increase your chances of winning. And yes, I shall drop the references to weapons right here and now in case it may offend certain folk.

The other instrument which I would wield alongside reading the fundamentals, would of course be that of using technical analysis, or chart reading, as some would call it. If fundamentals are able to provide the boundary for which you are able to herd and choose your companies, then technical analysis would give you the timing and signals to pull them out of the water and engage with them.

One gives you the system of filtration, the other gives you the system of engagement.

Let's have a look at what we usually look for in a company in order to determine if it has the potential to represent value.

Increasing Profits

Profits represent growth, and growth usually gives value and that translates to a winning investment for people like us investing in the stock market. What is better than profits? Well, increasing profits year on year. That would be great news actually to any vested person whose company is seeing such growth.

Usually, profit numbers can be easily gotten from the company's annual reports under the income statement portion. Most reports these days give at least a one-year comparison to the most recent set of reported figures, but that would not be sufficient. For the folks who deign not to use the power of the internet, they would then need to collate and flip through all the physical annual reports of the company for preferably ten years. If you can obtain fifteen, it would be even better. Remember, when we have more data, our brain acts like those of the artificial intelligence with their deep learning algorithms, we absorb and are able to process more.

I used to love to do that, because I just like to flip through reports. Something about the paper and the smell of it just drew me to it. I have to admit though, it was painstaking work. Honestly. After you went through three companies, you would probably start seeing stars. That is the reason why I would encourage all to utilize the technology that is available to us all. These days, you can easily take a look at the ten-year performance of a firm and zero in on its profit metric.

A good indicator would be a situation where you see year on year gradual, growth. This usually tells you that the company has got steady sales and at the same time, is also expanding to fill up the market potential. We would keep an eye out for the gross profit, while paying more attention to the net profit number. We want to see what the cost of sales and goods are to the company too. This way you would be able to figure out the company's margin and that can be a useful thing to have in your head.

When I see gradual growth, which is then punctuated by a sudden growth spurt, I have my sensors put out. To be honest, I don't really fancy such situations and would most definitely have to take a closer look at it. This is the time when you got to really go into the annual reports first, probably using at least three annual reports. I always take the preceding annual report, annual report for the growth spurt year, and the annual report after. You would want to investigate what was the cause of the growth spurt and the key question would be if it were sustainable. Many companies have such spurts on paper, and it shows up incredibly well, only to have it known later that profits were actually due to a one-off sale of some asset. It is our duty to find out what is happening, and make careful, factual judgements for ourselves, because it will build up our conviction when we go on to the decision-making phase.

Increasing Sales

The revenue or sales numbers are sometimes able to predict the profits because some industries record their sales numbers but do not book the profits until after the projects or goods are delivered. Sales numbers would be a good benchmark to assess any company and of course, we would want increasing sales year on year as evidence of having a growth company in our sights.

For some companies, their sales and profit numbers may register little or no growth, perhaps one or two percent per year. Counters like Macdonald's and General Electric would come into mind. These are more stable, steady counters that have engaged their market potential and are likely just to cruise along. What they represent to the investor would be cash in the forms of dividends as well as value creation via company stock buy backs. If well run, these behemoths usually would be sitting on stockpiles of cash, which are usually distributed as dividends to the shareholders or used in corporate stock purchases. Corporate stock purchases tend to boost the stock price per share because the purchases reduce the total number of shares available in the market.

Some would then ask, what would be the point of looking at such slow growing companies? Remember, our task is to pick and filtrate those companies which are well managed and are fitting to our criteria for being listed in our target pool. Though these bigger firms may not have the sales and profit growth figures, they do represent value when they have depressions in their stock prices due to either external or internal shocks. This is the reason why it would also be a good idea to have a handle of what would be a fair price for these stocks such that you would know if it's under or overvalued.

Chapter 17: Forex Vs. Stocks

For a long time, the accepted wisdom would have been to entrust your investment capital to some local brokerage service, and aside from browsing your regular monthly statements, that was the extent of your responsibilities. Very often an intelligent and clever person will start to contemplate whether they can handle helping to make their own investments, especially in the on-going economic crisis. Today, as a result of prevalent accessibility to electronic markets and software applications, just about anybody is able to get themselves into the market. Many, however, are intimidated by the mind-boggling complication and endemic corruption that prevails in the stock game, and many will probably take away that as a solution. There is another market, having said that, which provides the astute learner an arena into which they can safely venture. With all the self-esteem that the excellent schooling gives you, and the reassurance that a developed sense of discipline instills, the Forex market can be a dream become reality for the hopeful market warrior.

Convenient Accessibility

Probably the most enticing arguments that the Forex market is accessible to just about anyone is the fact that you can find virtually thousands of brokers that provide 100% Free of charge, no commitment, no deposit, down-loadable trading platforms that enable you to trade the market live employing a "demo" account. A Demo account provides you with almost identical experience that you will experience in case you at some point plan to start trading with actual money. The value of this type of practical experience is incalculable, mainly because it makes it possible for the trader to discover if or not he or she has got what it takes to contend in the world's greatest financial market. The ambitious trader can brainstorm, evaluate and test out methods for numerous days, months or years before they think they are really ready to get started. For the patient and disciplined, the value of this cannot be overstated.

Another advantage that the Forex market affords the amateur trader looking to uncover his niche may be the simplicity of entry into a live account. The playing field of stock trading is dominated by a select few online brokers who have jointly decided that $1,500 to $3,000 is apparently the minimal amount that they're going to settle for to open an account, and at those levels, the level of services is even decreased. In contrast, there are many reputable Foreign Exchange Brokers who have established Micro-lot programs which allow the trader to enter the marketplace with a very small level of risk by trading what is known as micro-lots. These programs extend their hand to the trader with minimal funds to use by minimizing the entry threshold to as small as $25.00. Moreover, these deposits can be achieved easily and quickly via a credit or debit card, while the vast majority of stock broker deposits require a wire transfer or ACH deposit.

One of several aggravating moments in a budding stock trader's career comes along at the time they figure out just how much funds they have to commit to a stock trade in order to earn substantial money on a shorter term move. As an example, to produce $500 on a 5% move over the course of one or two weeks, the trader needs to put in at a minimum $10,000 if he or she isn't margined. If margined at the ordinary maximum of 2 to 1, then that amount could be as low as $5,000, however the trader is exposed to the hazards inherent with being leveraged in the stock market. Sizable opening gaps and major surprise press releases can occur any time, and devastate the traders balance without giving that individual any possible way of avoiding the catastrophe. By comparison, the foreign exchange market supplies the trader a much reduced risk profile by offering as much as 500 to 1 leverage in certain marketplaces. A lot more reasonable would be the latest US standard of 50 to 1, but still, this amount of leverage enables a trader to drill right down to the lower time frames and develop a plan that extracts sizable gains from a considerably more tolerable risk profile. And, considering that the Forex market trades 24x7 during the weeks' time without any gaps, the probability is narrow that price will move substantially distant from the trader's entry price before they are able to make an exit determination. As long as the clever Currency trader exits trades on Friday, and enters again following the Sunday night EST opening time, the chances of getting burned by way of a gap or excessive flash move are very low.

On a similar wave link as the preceding point, the Forex market permits the trader to enter and exit in an unfettered manner, whatever the size or configuration of their account. On the other hand, the US stock markets require a participant to maintain an account balance with a minimum of $25,000 in their trading account to become classified and permitted as a "day trader". Without this kind of classification, you're going to be limited by 3 in/outs per 5 day rolling week, meaning that you are eligible to enter and exit within the same market session, but only three times every five day rolling week. This constraint causes fresh market participants to miss out on some of the most dependable setups that exist in the stock exchange, as they are not legally in a position to routinely enter and exit during the same day. Forex is victorious again!

"Technically" more accurate

Apart from the entrance requirements with regard to trading a live account, the Forex market provides the novice trader a not so steep learning curve than does the stock exchange. Simply because Forex trades at any hour, and traders are not "in a hurry" to sell or buy before an upcoming close in the marketplace, market players don't usually generate unreasonable movements that can't be predicted. The stock exchange, with its' pre-market, New york open, lunchtime doldrums, bond closings, NY close, and post-market trading produce a maze of motions that people outside the Wall Street Elite are left to simply make educated guesses about. The Currency markets, although it does react powerfully to some news items and from time to time does something that seems out of nowhere, generally gives the qualified trader intelligent and definable patterns with which to measure entries, stops and take profit levels. Forex, like every markets, enters into sideways patterns that are difficult to forecast, but, just like all markets, that's not the time to trade heavily. When the Forex market starts to trend, however, the proficient player is much like the proverbial "kid in a candy store" looking at and scooping up those little green and red candies.

The size of the Forex market is not able to even be fairly compared to the stock market. Nearly $4 trillion every day will be exchanged, and if you relate those dollars to the example of each and every one as being a vote, then it may help one comprehend the realities. Each and every one of those trades is a vote about what the present valuation on each currency set really should be, and the simple fact is that having such a huge ocean of variant thoughts about where the rate should be offers a dampening effect that results in a softer all around price movement. The effect can result in a more foreseeable and playable market.

In the stock exchange, the volume of shares on the market to trade of any one security will surely have an enormous impact on the way in which that security trades. The smaller the float, the more erratic and unforeseen its' movements can be. A lot of day traders don't like trading anything that trades less than 1 million shares every day. This method insures that the instrument is fluid enough for them to enter and exit with an acceptable degree of slippage. Compare and contrast that with the Forex market, where 4 million times that amount of dealings take place. To a Forex trader who eliminates trading news events and the 5pm EST carry over, slippage should really be wholly restricted to the market spread at the time of entry and exit.

That leads to one more reason that Forex makes sense as a trading vehicle for the rational trader, the reduced expenses of commission rates. In fact, hardly any Forex brokers even command commissions, as the primary revenue stream for a trustworthy Forex broker is the "pip spread". This is the difference between the typical bid and offer that is present with every market, however in Forex, that's everything that you "pay", although you never really write a check or see it subtracted from your account. The spread just gets folded into the trade, whether it profits or loses, so that when you exit all trades and your account is flat, the balance that shows in your balance is all yours. There is going to be no extra broker service fees, SEC fees, Exchange fees, data fees, etc... Now that's something that you are certain to get pumped up about.

Instruction can be acquired, but Buyer Beware!

Needless to say, it would be nearly impossible to find anyone who would consent that just anyone can enter in the market profitably without first obtaining a proper education. Despite the fact that, in rare instances, this has been accomplished, even then it wasn't without a variety of "near financial death" experiences, and very hard won lessons. Training is vital to successfully manage in the worlds' largest market, but where should an ambitious trader go to obtain the best instruction as well as the very best dollar value?

At this time there undoubtedly are a large number of operations on the net that claim to be able to convert the beginner trader into a professional in "just one weekend" or after "learning the secret that no one else knows"! Level headed individuals can detect these fraudsters a considerable way off, but others haven't been so fortuitous. The best advice will be to limit the level of funds you invest in instruction in the beginning, since trading capital is easily the most priceless asset that every trader has.

Chapter 18: Finding a Suitable Market

Once you get started trading stocks you will hear the phrase, "you are only as good as the stocks that you trade" often. According to many day trading experts, there is a lot of truth to this phrase. However, this phrase should not scare you away from day trading. Every beginner is unaware of what the best stocks are for their business at first. I want to help you learn what the best stocks are so you can get the best experience out of your day trading business from the beginning.

This is not to say that you aren't going to make mistakes. However, you shouldn't dwell on the mistakes you make in your business. Instead, you want to learn from them so you can step into the future of your day trading business with more experience and a lesson learned. You should also remember that even some of the most experienced day traders make mistakes. But, the more you take the time to learn about your new career, the fewer mistakes you will make along the way.

Just like any job, you want to make money consistently. Therefore, you need to pick stocks that are going to move and have enough volume. If you don't focus on these stocks, then you have wasted a trading day, made very little money, or even lost money.

Selecting the Best Stocks to Trade

Selecting the right stocks for your trades can be some of the toughest decisions you will make throughout your day. You will start this process right away in the morning as you catch up on the news and see what has changed in the stock market overnight. You will use your education, techniques, and other knowledge to go through and find a few stocks that pique your interest as a possible trade that day.

One of the most important factors to remember before you select is that you want to make sure you believe this stock is going to give you a sizable profit. Think of it this way: you can purchase a stock for $15 and then within five minutes sell the stock with a profit of $500. For many people, this is more money than they make in their usual day job in one day and you just made it within five minutes.

While this example isn't how most of your trades will happen, it is possible. You just have to make sure that you follow the steps, learn as much as you can, and follow the basics that are written in this book and elsewhere about day trading. You will also want to realize that you will not become a success overnight. In fact, it can take months before you start to see a good profit.

But still, this does not answer what type of stocks you can select as a day trader. While I can't tell you what specific stocks will be best for you (as only you can decide that), I can give you a brief list of some of the stocks you will run into as a day trader that seem to be on the popular lists.

Penny Stocks

Penny stocks are an option you can consider. These stocks are not very popular and they tend to be a part of the market where most day traders don't look. However, these stocks are some of the cheapest to buy, and although they are typically over a penny, they tend to be under $1 each. At the same time, many of these stocks tend to not trade for more than $5. This can still give you a good profit if you invest in the right penny stocks. The trick is understanding the details of penny stocks in order to gain the best profit from them.

At the same time, penny stocks can give you a large capital loss. This is because the companies that go in the penny stocks category are the ones who aren't doing the best and hope to make some money through investments made in their company. This can often work out better for the company than it does the trader, mostly because the company will gain the money you put into the stock, whereas you could end up losing money on your trade.

Because of this, you want to make sure you understand what company you are purchasing from if you decide to get into penny stocks. If you know how to handle penny stocks and the company seems to be on the more successful side, then you are more likely to gain a profit than receive a loss. However, it is not just the company you want to become aware of when if you trade in penny stocks.

You also want to make sure that you know where you heard about the penny stocks. Unfortunately, like other areas in the world, the stock market is full of people who are trying to scam other people out of money one way or another. Some of these people will focus on penny stocks. They will purchase tons of penny stocks and then make fake news releases or post untrue information about how well the company of the penny stock is doing. They will talk about how if you purchase some of these stocks you will be able to end your day with a huge profit. However, because there is no hard truth in what they are saying, you could well end up with a loss at the end of the day instead of a profit. This is another reason why it is extremely important to make sure you do your research before you take on any stock or other investment.

Stocks in Play

This is a popular phrase that day trader often uses. Stocks in play refer to stocks which have great reward opportunities. However, because of this, they can also have higher risk than other stocks. Due to this, it is best that beginners gain a little trading experience before they start looking at stocks in play.

Stocks in play will change daily, which tends to be a benefit for day traders. All the stocks included in stocks in play allow you to become efficient with your buying power, which is one of the best ways to earn a profit.

How can you find stocks in play? There are actually several avenues that allow you to find stocks that are included in this category. For example, stocks that have fresh news, a stock that has increased or decreased around 2% right before the market opened for the day, or a stock that has great intraday levels.

SPDR S&P 500 ETF

The SPDR is one of the hottest stocks on the market in 2019. Whether you are more interested in investing or you are a day trader, this is a common stock to see. When it comes to trading, the SPDR receives over 100 million trades a day, and it is known to generate pretty good profits.

While this might seem like the right investment for a day trader as many people feel it almost guarantees a profit, you still want to make sure that it fits in with your strategy. On top of this, you will want to follow your trading plan before purchasing this stock. Even if the stock is known as one of the most popular stocks with good profit, you will still want to make sure it fits your plan, your strategy, and your style as a trader.

Successful Companies Often Mean Popular Day Trade Stocks

Some of the most common stocks people look at as day traders are also some of the most popular companies. For example, JCPenney, Facebook, and Yahoo! often top the lists. While these stocks are popular because of the benefits and gains that day, traders tend to receive from them, this doesn't mean that you want to jump on these stocks to start with. As stated before, you want to make sure that it fits into your plan, strategy, and every other facet of your trading scheme before you decide to take on any of the more popular stocks.

On top of this, for day traders, some of the most popular companies can also have larger risks than other companies. Because of this, you are going to want to make sure that the stock fits into your level of risk before you make any type of purchase or trade.

Factors to Help You Select the Best Stocks

In order to help you find the best stocks for yourself, you need first to develop your trading plan. This is the plan you will follow throughout your career. You will also review this plan often.

Another developmental step you will want to focus on before you dive into the market is to make sure that you have chosen your strategy and you have a thorough understanding your strategy. You need to make sure that you know your strategy well, because you will often have to quickly think when it comes to analyzing a stock and whether it will work with your strategy or not.

Once you get through the basics of starting up your trading business, then you can start focusing on what type of stocks you will look for.

Volatility and Volume

Volatility is a mathematical measurement that you will want to complete in order to help you determine what types of returns you will receive from a specific stock. One of the keys rules to remember when it comes to volatility is the higher the measurement, the riskier the stock will be.

When we discuss volume in the stock market, we are referring to the number of shares that were traded throughout the day. You will pay a lot of attention to volume when you get into the technical analysis part of your day trading career.

Both volume and volatility are important when you are looking for what type of stock to watch to see if it is something you will be interested in purchasing or trading. Of course, you will always want to watch the guidelines and factors that you set for yourself in your business plan, such as your risk level and the amount of volume you feel comfortable with.

If you are a trader who is more interested in your stock moving slowly, then you will want to focus on stocks that have higher volume than volatility. However, if you want to focus on stocks where the prices tend to increase and decrease rapidly, then you will look in another direction when picking your stock.

It is important to note that no matter what stock you are looking at, volatility and volume are going to change over time. This is a natural process of the trading world and one that you will become used to. In fact, it is through these two factors that you will begin analyzing the stocks you are looking at to gauge your interest level in taking on these stocks.

Chapter 19: Stock Market Technical Analysis

When it comes to ensuring that your successful trade percentage only increases as time goes on, you may find it useful to branch out of analyzing the fundamentals of a company to determine if its stock is worth considering and also to analyze it technically. Technical analysis studies past market trends with the goal of accurately predicting those that are likely to occur again in the future. Technical analysis is ideal for those that like the idea of determining future performance by looking at previous prices, without having to dig through mountains of paperwork to find the details you are looking for. While the past will never be able to predict the future 100 percent of the time truly, technical analysis is useful when combined with a basic understanding of market mentality for generating predictions that are accurate within reason.

Core assumptions

The goal of technical analysis is not to simply measure the given intrinsic value of a particular currency, but rather to use the tools at your disposal to pick out beneficial patterns related to a future activity that others may not yet have noticed. At its core, technical analysis functions by assuming 3 things to be true. First, the market will always discount anything; second, prices will always move according to trends; and finally, history will always repeat itself eventually.

The market will always discount everything

While detractors say that technical analysis is only concerned with the movement of currency price and little else; in reality, technical analysis assumes that the current price of a currency is a reflection of everything that is going on that could possibly affect that currency which then makes it an accurate way to assess overall value. This is then taken into account along with the broader economic climate as well as the current phase to determine when a valuable opportunity comes along.

Price will always move according to trends

If the current value or price of a given currency is said to move according to an established trend, this means that once you can clearly determine a trend when it comes to past currency performance you have a much greater chance of seeing that same trend repeat itself when compared to the chances of an entirely new trend, or the opposite trend occurring instead. Technical trading strategies tend to assume that this is always the case if they are going to work effectively.

History will repeat itself eventually

If prices move in trends, then it naturally stands to reason that technical analysis believes that as far as currency prices go, history will always repeat itself. This can be chalked up to the fact that those who participate in the market are likely always to respond the same way to similar market movement. This is often plotted using chart patterns in an effort to determine these trends at their start when they can be capitalized on to the fullest. While some of these charts have been in use for over a century, they are still relevant when it comes to how the public reacts to price changes.

Price charts

A price chart is a core part of technical analysis; essentially, it is a chart with both an x and a y-axis where the price can be seen along the vertical axis and the time can be seen along the horizontal axis. While there are plenty of different charts to choose from, each with their own unique strengths and weaknesses, those that you will want to keep in mind early on include the line chart, the candlestick chart, the bar chart, and the point and click chart.

Line chart

The line chart is the simplest of all the charts because all it does is showing the closing price of a given stock over a set period of time. The lines, in this case, are formed once the grouping of closing prices has been determined and then connected with the end goal of showing a trend. You won't be able to find details such as what the opening price for the same period of time was or what the overall results for the day were but you will be able to determine if the day over day is positive, which is still quite important, which is why this is one of the first charts that day traders of all skill levels consult when they are looking into the details of a new stock.

Candlestick chart

Another worthwhile technical analysis tool that you are going to want to be familiar with is the candlestick. They provide important data for traders across multiple time frames by creating what is known as price bars. Each day will provide you with details regarding the high, open, close and low points of the stock each day. These details can be used to build patterns that make it easier to predict how the price is likely going to move in the future.

The candlesticks that are going to be the most accurate when it comes to plotting the price of stocks are going to fall into two types, continuations and reversals. Reversal candlestick patterns tend to predict a coming change in the current pricing trends. Meanwhile, continuation patterns predict that the current price action is simply going to continue as is.

A candlestick chart is similar to a bar chart, though the information it provides is much more detailed overall. Like a bar chart, it includes a line to indicate the range for the day, however, when you are looking at a candlestick chart you will notice a wide bar near the vertical line which indicates the degree of difference the price saw throughout the day. If the price that the stock is trading at increases overall for the day, then the candlestick will often be clear while if the price has decreased then the candlestick is going to be red.

Point and figure chart

While the point and figure chart aren't used as much as it once was, it has been in use for more than 100 years which means there is still plenty of use left in it. The point and figure chart are useful when you want to know the movement of prices, without worrying about volume or time spent. This makes it a pure pricing indicator without much of the noise that many other charts need to deal with. It is also useful if the other types of charts contain information that is skewing them in one way or the other.

When you first see a point and figure chart you will always be able to tell because it is comprised of lines of Xs and Os instead of points and lines. In this instance, the Xs are going to indicate periods of positive trends while Os will represent downward trends. The numbers and letters along the bottom of the chart indicate months and date estimates. Point and click charts also include a set of reversal criteria that is set by the trader looking at the chart, these criteria consider the amount the price is going to move in order for an X to become an O or vice a versa. As the trend changes, it shifts right to indicate this fact.

Support and resistance

Understanding support and resistance is crucial to achieving the success you are looking for when it comes to technical analysis and while they may seem complex at first, they will become clearer every time you put the theory around them into practice. At their most basic, resistance can be thought of as the ceiling on the price of a particular currency or currency pair which means the price is unlikely to move past this point while support can be thought of as the price floor where it is unlikely to decrease any further.

Trend lines

While it is not uncommon for these ceilings and floors to change on a regular basis, being prepared for these changes is what separates the novice traders from the experts. Understanding these movements is done through the use of trend lines. When the market is trending upward then new resistance levels are going to be formed as that upward price movement begins to slow before starting its trek back down the trendline. This is likely to happen when uncertainty rises in regard to a given stock. This will, in turn, create what is known as a short-term top which is essentially a temporary price plateau in the overall movement pattern.

Shorter trends can actually be part of trends that are much longer overall, which is why it is important to always double check and ensure you aren't making a move on something that is only an offshoot of a much larger, and much different trend. To make the process of deciding what's what even easier, it is important to always keep an eye on the weekly, daily and yearly charts if you want to locate any truly long-term trends. If you are looking to get rich quick, however, then you will want to stick to the daily charts instead.

After you have found an especially interesting trend, the next step is going to be drawing a trendline that is as simple as drawing a straight line that correctly illustrates the direction the trend is currently moving in. When it comes to an uptrend, you will want to draw your line in such a way that it connects the dots of all of the lows in such a way that the line is below the relevant data. If you are looking at a reversal trend then you are going to want to draw the line so that it connects the highs, leaving the data below the trendline.

It is important to start paying extremely close attention to the price of the stock that you are watching when it begins to reach again the point where the trendline begins to broaden as this is likely to be the point where the price is going to cease its downward fall. It is important to note in instances such as this that a trendline can lend support to a given stock for a significant period of time while changing very little in the interim. Likewise, if the market is in a downward trend overall then you will want to be on the lookout for a set of peaks at a declining angle and a trendline that connects the point of each peak together. As the price gets closer to the trendline you are going to want to be on the lookout for indicators that point towards selling as this is how the price was likely pushed lower previously as well.

You will also want to keep an eye out for channel lines which are a pair of lines to the side of the data you are watching that indicate the levels of resistance and support that are in play. One trendline connects the highs while the other connects the lows while the resulting channel can either go up or down, or even sideways, but the interpretation will always remain constant. The goal should be to establish a channel that is long enough to show a break from the data that it has been following. This breakout point will mark the best time to get in on the trend you are following to ensure that you have the maximum amount of time to profit from the trend you have discovered.

Chapter 20: Pros and Cons

If investing in stock were easy, everyone would invest. Stock requires some time, dedication, and education before beginning. There are several reasons why individuals choose never to start investing in stock. Despite these reasons, many enjoy their stock investments and receive quite a nice profit from their investments. There are several reasons why a stock is the best way to invest your money, and there are several reasons why some choose not to invest in stock. Financial goals will differ from person to person, which is why it's crucial to learn both the pros and cons of stock. Recognizing the pros and cons will allow investors to be further educated on the stock market. It will also help investors to recognize the ways to use their money better. There are also many types of different investments and places to put one's money. The individual may opt to put their money in a bank account, invest it in real estate, purchase bonds, or purchase other tangible assets. These are all ways to use one's money, and they all have their advantages and disadvantages. Depending on the goals of the investor, there may be a better choice for the individual.

Stock: Pros and Cons

There are several ways in which stock investments are amazing; there are also some not-so-amazing aspects of stock. It is crucial to understand these aspects to further one's knowledge about stocks.

Stock is incredible in many ways. It is a great way to sit back and take advantage of the growth occurring in the economy. Over time, most companies will experience growth. Stocks allow investors to take advantage of that growth present in the economy. Additionally, stocks allow stockholders to keep up with (and stay ahead of) inflation. While inflation averages a rate of about 3.2% per year, stock averages a return of around 10% per year, that's over triple the amount! That is, however, over the longer-term. Throughout the year, stock greatly fluctuates. Yet, stock gives its investors very high returns, especially compared to other methods of investments and assets. In addition to the growth that stock offers, stockholders may enjoy the additional income given to them by dividends. Stock is also easy to buy. Because of the rise of online stockbrokers, stocks may be bought in seconds. Investing in stock is also highly customizable. The investor may choose which companies they wish to buy stock in, the amount they wish to buy of it, and how long they would like to hold on to it for. It is quite easy to diversify one's portfolio, and the options are seemingly limitless for what one may invest in. There are also several other options for buying stock. Stock is also very simple to sell. It may be sold within seconds online, and the money may be easily transferred to another account. If one needs their money quickly transferred to another account, that may be done easily. The costs of buying and selling stock are minimal, as there are typically only small fees for online transactions. Because of the ease of buying and selling stocks, stocks are highly liquid. They may easily be bought or sold, and they may be converted to cash quickly if the investor wishes to do so. Stock is also an easy way to take an ownership stake in companies. This may be only a very small portion of the company owned, yet it is quite simple to develop this relationship with the company as an owner. It may easily be stopped by selling the stocks, transferring that ownership to someone else.

Although the stock is a great way to invest one's money, there are a few disadvantages to stock investments. These must be addressed to understand the potential negative aspects of stock. However, stock investors understand these aspects, yet know that the advantages outweigh the disadvantages. Some disadvantages may also be avoided or minimized with further education. Stock is always a risk. Investors may easily lose their investment if the company does poorly enough. There may also be taxes to pay, which can further losses. If a company goes bankrupt, stockholders will be paid last. Stock is a time-consuming investment. It requires education, research, and management. Emotions may also get in the way of investments. A long-term professional trader knows not to get too caught up in the rises and falls of a stock, as it will even out over time. Day traders much dedicate their time to observing, measuring, and predicting these fluctuations, though. Stockholders tend to sell low due to fear and buy high due to greed. This is where emotions may prove detrimental to one's performance. There is also the "competition" between beginning investors and professionals. Without the proper knowledge and tools to invest, individuals will miss out on opportunities that they may have had access to otherwise. Stockholders are also competing with each other. A response to a prediction of a rise or fall can trigger a sharp rise or fall of stock, leading to the volatility of a stock. Stocks also require diversification, which may be a disadvantage if one wishes to only invest in one company or sector. If so, one risks losing all of their money in the case of economic misfortune. Those who pick the wrong stock may also suffer, as they will lose their investment in the case of poor performance.

Stocks vs. Bank Accounts

Much like stock, putting one's money into a bank account has its advantages and disadvantages. Much like stock, a bank account is a great place to hold money in and may easily be transferred to cash. The goals of both differ, however. Bank accounts serve the primary purpose of saving, while the stock market is more of an investing method. The best choice for the individual will depend on that individual's goals and financial situation. If the individual is already in debt, investing may not be the best idea. They may lose even more money than they have already lost. For those wishing to increase the amount of money that they have (and those who have the money to be able to invest), investing is wise and will yield a greater return. It is wise to diversify where one puts their money. Everyone should have some sort of emergency savings in case of job loss, medical issues, or another emergency. The typical amount to save is three months' worth of living expenses. It is also wise for those who are young to save for a house, school, and more. Those of all ages should begin saving for retirement as quickly as possible. There are always new items and services to buy, so one shouldn't wait until they want something to begin to save. A portion of each paycheck should go towards savings just in case. This will lead to a safe place for money to rest until it is spent. However, a portion of every paycheck should also go towards stocks. While one shouldn't spend all of their free money investing (just to be safe), it is wise to set aside money regularly towards investing. It is wise to take advantage of the greater return that stock provides, as opposed to leaving all of one's money in a savings account. Whereas bank accounts are generally stagnant, stocks will increase in value over time and provide many stockholders with dividends. This leads to a much greater return, as stockholders receive a 10% return on average. The typical bank account provides the user with under 1% interest. However, one must consider risk. While most bank accounts are risk-free, stock investments always come with a risk. One may select a stock that has been less risky historically, yet there may always be a slight risk. This risk is generally offset by the gains resulting from investing, though. Additionally, both investing and saving are quite easy. Because of financial operations transitioning to an online setup, transactions are quick and easy. It may take time to learn how both are set up, yet it is quite easy once one learns the system. Both offer many variations. With stock, one may invest in a variety of companies in many ways. They may also keep that stock for whichever period of time that they choose. There are many brokers out there, and one may hire an investment advisor. The same goes for saving in a banking institution. There are many banks, types of bank accounts, and options for financial advisors. There are many options for bank accounts.

A savings account is a typical account for those wishing to save their money. They have very little interest, usually only a portion of a percent. They are risk-free and easy to maintain, although they do not provide anywhere close to the return that stock does. It is possible to have an online banking account as well as a physical bank account, and many offer the ability to perform transactions online. However, some services may need to occur in a physical location, which may not be as convenient as an online service.

Checking accounts are not primarily used for savings; these are accounts that are primarily focused on a continuous flow of money in and then back out. It is easy to deposit money and checks, withdraw, and make payments from these accounts. It is also easy to transfer money in and out of these accounts. However, checking accounts typically have no interest, unlike stock investments. They certainly don't pay out dividends! They do, however, usually come with a debit card, which can be quite efficient for transactions. Although they do usually involve fees, if one overdraws their account, that will incur fees. There may also be maintenance fees and minimum balances required.

Money market accounts are ways of earning a bit higher interest than a typical savings account. However, they typically require a minimum balance. Plus, they may require fees, and the interest rates aren't usually very high. There may also be a limited amount of withdrawals per month, which may prove beneficial for those trying to save their money. This is another way to save money, though, and there is typically no risk involved.

A CD account (certificate of deposit) is the bank account with the highest interest rate, yet there is a catch. The individual will not have access to that money for the time period in which they hold it in that CD. This is good for extra money that doesn't need to be accessed, yet that money would do much better in stock investment. Although the rates are higher than a typical bank account, they still rest at about 1-5%, which does not yield nearly as much as the typical 10% return enjoyed by stockholders. The benefit, though, is the no-risk element of such accounts.

The final main type of bank account is the broad area of retirement accounts. These include IRAs and such. These are great ways to save for retirement and enjoy the tax benefits of such accounts. These accounts may also require those that hold them to not have access to their money for a certain period of time, whereas stock may be easily sold and converted to cash.

Chapter 21: The Fundamentals of the Stock Market

The right investment attitude, essentially, is a blend of six key characteristics. Over time, it is the right contributing approach that will have the impact between an acceptable auditor and a dependably productive financial expert.

What do we understand by the expression "Contributing Mindset?" Essentially, it is about the mental and intellectual nature of the financial expert. Remember, contributing is as a lot of a mental intermingling as it is a series of skill and data. To be sure, even with the best of abilities and all-around data, you are most likely not going to win as a fiscal expert if you don't have the right contributing viewpoint. The right risk perspective, essentially, is a blend of six key characteristics. Over time, it is the right contributing attitude that will have the greatest impact upon developing the skills of a good financial expert and a consistently productive auditor.

Mental balance is the key

What do we fathom by mental prudence? It is the ability to think indisputably despite when markets are unusual and the financial expert is under tremendous weight. Usually, this is when most financial expert will as a rule sway and accept veritable contributing failures. Believe it or not, mental aptitude is about the calm that you can keep up despite when the market appears to go against you. There are extremely two perspectives to mental balance. Stock exchanges are driven by fear and insatiability. Ordinarily, financial experts will when all is said in done get energetic at the most elevated purpose of the market and terrible at the base of the market. Smart contributing is connected to doing the cautious reverse. For example, if you had kept up your balance at the market lows of 2003 and 2009, by then you would have ended up with surprising assumptions at remarkable costs.

Not just peace of mind; you also require balance

How definitely is balance unique in connection to peace of mind? What makes a difference is extremely unnoticeable, however, notwithstanding all that it exists. For example, self-restraint is connected to being terrible or greedy in the business sectors at the opportune times. If you get this mix wrong, you could end up with mishaps. Parity is about the point of view wherein you take decisions. A segment of the basic principles are: avoid choosing huge endeavor decisions when you are in a state of ire or dissatisfaction; similarly, avoid investment decisions when you are in a state of uneasiness or doubt; above all, keep away from taking authentic venture decisions in a state of vitality, since you are well while in transit to overextend yourself.

Do whatever it takes not to seek after returns, seek after the right framework.

If you are more focused on the results rather than the technique, if you are more worried over the closures than about the strategies, by then you have an attitude problem with respect to contributing. Remember, contributing is substantially more of getting the framework right. How you recognize stocks, how you screen stocks, what are the non-cash related parameters you consider, how might you impact on the channel and the boundaries of security, how might you incorporate a motivation by aligning your passage and leave levels; all these are a bit of your methodology or system. Your consideration should be on fulfilling this methodology and the results will thusly come after.

Act generally determined and be a self-motivated student

The stock exchange is a remarkable teacher yet to really take in the fundamental activities from the market, you should be an excited observer and a self-motivated student. The best way to deal with gain from the market is to listen energetically to what the market is trying to tell you. Endeavor to record the learnings from the market consistently and it can transform into your Bible for exchanging. The embodiment of the issue is that your viewpoint should be that of a self-student. The market isn't the place you will be demonstrated the nuances. It is a monstrous gathering of data from which you can liberally draw upon.

Be humble to recognize challenges and your mistakes

If you don't practice calmness in your practices, then contributing isn't for you. The best of financial experts gets their assumptions wrong. Attempt to be humble enough to concede that you weren't right and make appropriate helpful change (s). If pride drives you to either average the position or outflank the market, by then you will have a certifiable attitude problem when you are contributing. Recognize that the market has a lot to demonstrate to you and recognize your mistakes. That is the route in to the right contributing attitude.

An ounce of movement justifies a pound of orchestrating

You can make the best of plans within the planning stage before trading. There are a couple of things about the stock exchanges that you can adjust just once you start exchanging with real money. Amusement can simply take you so far! Grasp a frame of mind that is action planned rather than delighting a great deal in craftiness. Finally, that is what makes a difference!

The 4 Different Money Mindsets of Investing

1) People Who Prefer to Give Their Investing Capital to Someone Else.

These individuals are deliberately missing out on contributing, in light of the fact that they recognize that they are occupied with different things that are otherwise important to them.

In this manner, they give their cash to a common investment manager and take essential money management plan from somebody who gets you a 3% return on your cash. You surely aren't getting the advantages you merit by having another person deal with your cash and you completely don't have the foggiest idea of where your money is invested.

2) People Who Don't Want to Learn to Invest

They don't recognize they can do it; these individuals are purposefully careless about contributing in light of the way that they trust it's difficult to learn or not worth the work.

The marvelous thing about following up on profits is that it continues working when you aren't. You need to invest some work directly, yet over time you essentially find the opportunity to watch your cash make in profits.

3) People Who Have No Money (Or Think They Don't Have Enough Money)

These people think they need money to be an analyst and are coincidentally do not participate in the process of investing money. You can make sense of how to contribute without a tremendous measure of money. I've clarified the most ideal approach is to save $500 to begin investing.

The cash related trade recommends the group of business segments and trades where regular exercises of purchasing, selling, and issuance of bits of openly held companies occur. Such financial activities are exchanged with customary trades or over-the-counter (OTC) business centers which work under a depicted plan of principles. There can be unmistakable stock trading locales in a nation or a country, which permit trades stocks and different sorts of stock.

Regardless of how it is known as a cash related trade or financial element and is basically known for trading stocks/values, other financial affirmations - like Exchange Traded Funds (ETF), corporate securities and reinforcements dependent on stocks, commodities, financial structures, and insurances - are additionally exchanged the investments trades.

Understanding the Stock Market

While today it is conceivable to buy about everything on the web, there is consistently a consigned market for everything. For example, individuals drive to city borders and farmlands to buy Christmas trees, visit the nearby timber market to purchase wood and other essential material for home merchandise and revamps, and go to investments like Walmart for their standard basic sustenance commodities supplies.

Such committed markets fill in as a stage where various purchasers and merchants meet, group up, and execute. Since the measure of market people is a lot, one is guaranteed of a reasonable cost. For instance, if there is just a single seller of Christmas trees in the whole city, he will have the chance to charge any amount he feels satisfied with, and the purchasers won't have any place else to go. Perhaps the number of tree dealers is great in a standard business center; they fight with one another to draw in purchasers. The purchasers will be overwhelmed to make decision with low-or limited faultless regarding making it a reasonable market in relation to openness. Without a doubt, even while shopping on the web, purchasers' separate costs offered by various brokers on a practically identical shopping path or transversely over various ways to get the best arrangements, persuading the particular online sellers to offer the best cost.

A cash related trade is an equal given market for trading different sorts of confirmations in a controlled, secure, and known environment. Since the investments trade joins an enormous number of market people who wish to purchase and sell shares, it guarantees reasonable surveying practices and openness in trades. While prior securities trades used to issue and plan in paper-based physical deal confirmations, the moved PC helped cash related trades work electronically.

How the Stock Market Works

Practically, insurances trades give a protected and composed condition where market people can execute in shares and other qualified financial instruments with sureness with zero-to low-operational risk. Working under the depicted guidelines as imparted by the controller, the financial trades known as crucial markets and as optional markets.

As an essential market, the investments trade enables relationship to issue and offer their plans to the standard open, through the procedure of Initial Public Offerings (IPO). This movement engages relationship to raise noteworthy capital from experts. In a general sense, it gathers that an affiliation disengages itself into various shares (state, 20 million shares) and sells a touch of those shares (state, 5 million shares) to customary open at a value (state, $10 per share).

To support this method, a company needs a business model where these shares can be sold. This business model is given by the stock exchange. If everything goes as per the plans, the company will successfully sell the 5 million shares at a cost of $10 per offer and accumulate $50 million financial profits. Financial experts will get the company shares which they can plan to hold for their favored length, completely anticipating rising in share cost and any potential compensation as benefit portions. The stock exchange goes about as a facilitator for this capital raising methodology and gets a charge for its organizations from the company and its cash related accessories.

Chapter 22: Beginners Mistakes

Investing in the stock market can be exciting. It can also generate feelings of fear and despair. These emotional rollercoasters can lead new investors into making bad decisions. Many new investors also fail to educate themselves about how the markets work and the things they need to pay attention to. We all make mistakes, and these factors and more can lead to costly mistakes that lead to loss of capital. However, if you take some time to educate yourself and prepare ahead of time, you can minimize your mistakes and the costs of mistakes that you do make.

Prepare Before You Start Investing

Many people who decide they want to get into the stock market are anxious to do so. However, it's important to prepare before you start buying shares. The first thing that every person should do is make sure that they have an emergency fund of cash stashed away, and that you will not use it to buy stocks or to cover losses. The purpose of an emergency fund is to have money on hand in case you hit the skids with a job or lose other sources of income if you have a car or medical emergency, or your basement floods and you need to pay for expensive home repairs. Recent surveys have shown that far too many Americans have been neglecting basic savings, and many could not even meet a $400 emergency car repair. If you are in a situation where you couldn't pay for a $400 car repair, then you are not quite ready to get into the stock market. You should work to save up a little bit of money first. Many experts recommend that you save up around six months of required funds to pay all your living expenses, and that is good advice, however that doesn't mean you have to wait that long to start investing, but you should at least get two months ahead before you start buying stocks.

Another important part of preparation is education. And congratulations, by reading this book, you've demonstrated that you are the kind of person who is willing to take time to learn before jumping into something! That is a very important consideration, especially when money is involved. You should also look into courses that are available online and read as many books as possible, especially when trying to determine what kind of risks you are willing to take and how to marry your investment goals with that. There are many online courses available on basic stock investing, day trading, swing trading, options, and other topics. There are even many good videos you can watch on YouTube to get a grasp of many of the basic topics.

In recent years the development of simulators is one of the most exciting tools for education. These can be really useful, especially if you've never done self-directed investing before, but especially for those who are looking to be day traders, swing traders, or trade options. Practice makes perfect as they say, and that's as true with investing and trading as it is with anything else. If it's important for a football player to practice before a game, it's important for a new trader to practice day trading or options trading, before putting real money on the line.

Investing or Trading Based on Emotions Rather Than Facts

One problem with investing and trading are that emotions ride high. It's completely natural to experience emotional highs and lows as the stock market does its usual roller coaster ride. However, what you don't want to do is let emotions start guiding your decisions and taking you over.

The process of being guided by emotion can start at the very beginning when you choose your very first stock to invest in. Ask yourself a question – why are you choosing that particular company? Are you picking different companies because you think they are cool, or because you are really taking a cold hard look at company fundamentals? You should be selecting companies based on whether or not they meet your investment goals. So you should be looking at their earnings, their future prospects, the P/E ratio and other important metrics that will help you decide whether or not a company is 1) in good shape both now and for the long term future as far as you can see it, and 2) that the company actually helps you meet your investment goals.

Maybe you are in love with Apple. But being in love with Apple is not a good enough reason to buy stock in Apple. If Apple doesn't match up with your investment goals, you should be looking elsewhere.

Emotion has a huge influence when people are facing losses. People panic and sell off. When the Dow Jones starts declining, people start moving their cash into "safe" investments, many that these days don't even pay hardly anything like money market funds. Some people don't even do that and just sell out and take the cash.

As an investor, you need to be disciplined. The courses of action described in the last paragraph that is governed by fear and panic are not the courses of action that a disciplined investor is going to take. Now if you are a swing trader and the market is declining, then either you're going to sell, or you're going to be shorting the stock. If you are a long-time investor, however, you most certainly shouldn't follow the lemmings over the cliff. What you should be doing is looking at a downturn as a buying opportunity. So, you should be loading up on shares, but don't do it all at once. When the market enters a downturn, nobody can be sure how low it's going to go, so you want to make disciplined, periodic purchases the way you always do. Dollar cost averaging always works when you are in it for the long haul. That doesn't mean you won't miss some opportunities, but over time the market will rebound again, and by the time you are in your retirement years, the prices will be much higher than they were when you originally invested in most cases.

There are going to be some cases when you're going to want to bail. An individual stock can decline for many reasons, and sometimes there is a point of no return. For example, Bear Sterns crashed from $170 a share to $2 a share over a matter of a few weeks. If you had invested in Bear Sterns, then you should have been studying the situation closely and you would have gotten out early.

So, you might want to bail from an individual stock when the data tells you that this is the right course of action. But you never get out of any stock simply based on panic. Know what the fundamentals are of the company.

Emotion works the other way too. When it seems like a stock simply goes up and up, people can start getting giddy about it. You might be tempted to put your entire life savings into that one stock. But that is a bad idea, no matter how good the stock is. As we've mentioned before, it's great to know that Amazon increased so much that an investment of a few thousand would have made you a millionaire, but hindsight is 20/20. Right now, it's impossible to know which if any social media companies are going to actually bank profits and still be around in 20 years, so it would be foolish to put your life savings into one. The so-called investor who goes around claiming to know what the next sure thing is can be called nothing more than a fool.

Another problem is people get emotionally invested in one company. Maybe it's because of the mission of the company or the products it makes that people think are going to "change the world." But when you get emotionally invested in a company, you start becoming irrational. Good examples include Tesla and Theranos. Let's take the latter case. Theranos claimed to have invented a revolutionary means to let people test their blood and to have medications delivered. It became clear that it was a sham, but the people who were emotionally invested in the company and the female CEO were literally fooled about it – and some still are even though it's clear now that Theranos is done and the CEO may even be facing charges.

In the case of Tesla, the jury is still out. They make high-quality products but have problems with delivery and scaling. They may yet overcome those problems. But if you talk to many Tesla investors, they are zealots about it. If Tesla ends up going down the drain, many of the investors may go down with it. Is it worth it?

To avoid letting emotion take over whether you get swept up with the lemmings running off the cliff when there is a bear market, whether you panic when an individual stock starts dropping, or whether you get hyper-excited when your favorite company is booming, you need to have rules in place beforehand and follow them.

For example, one rule that you could have in place is you never invest more than 5% of your portfolio in any single company. If you do that, then you are not going to be damaged even if you're a bit taken in by the company or you panic when it drops – or worse – miss when you should get out. Think about the poor fools who stayed invested in Bear Sterns until the end, and even the government wouldn't bail them out.

This is one reason why I like ETFs, although you don't have to use them for your entire portfolio. They divorce you from the problems that can arise when you start getting emotionally invested in one stock.

Putting Too Much Stake in the past Performance

One mistake many new (and even experienced) investors make is putting too much credence in the past performance of a stock. The fact is, as they say in the disclaimer, past performance is not a guarantee of future returns.

So, people often look at past performance as a guarantee of future performance when history shows that it is more often than not, simply not true. So, you might've seen a run-up of some particular stock over the last year, maybe it was Netflix, or maybe it was Amazon. And so, you just expected to continue. Of course, the real world doesn't work that way and the expected returns may not materialize. As it is, although none of us can tell the future, the run-ups of Netflix and Amazon may have come to an end. Of course, over the very long term, we probably expect both of those to grow. We simply don't know, so putting all of your investments into Netflix isn't a good idea, but you might want to put some of your investments into Netflix.

So, let's take Apple as another example. Apple has had an incredible run up over the past 10 to 12 years. Ever since they introduced the first iPhone, growth has been spectacular, expectations have been high, and returns have been even better. We really haven't seen anything quite like it before.

Chapter 23: Mindset and Psychology

Traders must have a certain mindset when it comes to investing. Investing in stock takes a lot of self-discipline. There is a certain psychology that traders must become familiar with to be successful in their investments. There is a whole investing mindset that must be utilized to drive results. Investors must detach themselves from their emotions when investing in stock; otherwise, they risk trading out of fear and greed. Investors must also not become too attached to any stock. Although there is an art to investing, it is important that investors utilize logic to drive their actions.

Self-Discipline

Self-discipline is crucial when it comes to investing. Investors must be able to follow their plans and achieve their goals. However, many investors become tempted by the idea of better performance and abandon all logic in hopes of achieving greater returns on their investments. They will use emotions when it comes to market conditions. They may also incur greater costs because of a lack of discipline. Investors must stick with their original plan despite temptations otherwise. A short-term sacrifice will be worth it in the long-term. Although it may not be the most appealing path, the disciplined path is most often the most successful path, especially when it comes to trading.

Following the original plan and goals that the investor set is crucial. Although there are situations in which it may be more beneficial to adjust the plans due to a highly changing market or personal financial misfortune, it is better to stick to the original plan most of the time. Once the investor strays from the path originally, it will become easier to repeat that action and abandon all original plans. The investor may act without using logic and end up incurring great losses. When this happens, however, investors fail to see the consequences of their actions in the long-term. Stocks that the investors should have held onto could have resulted in gains, but the investor chose to incur losses because of a lack of discipline instead. The investor opens themselves up to allowing for loopholes whenever they deem necessary, and they hurt themselves in the long-term. The investor should create a plan for what to do if the market is negative and stick to this. They should create this plan beforehand so that they are not biased at all. However, the real discipline is actually following through with this plan when the time comes.

The investor should also be disciplined in their amount of investments. Instead of deciding last-minute use the money that they planned to set aside for stock on spending, they should stick to the original plan. It is quite easy to say that one will not invest this week and get right back to it the next week, but they have already fallen off of the plan. This can discourage the investor and lead to further lack of discipline in the future. The best way to avoid this from happening is to stick with the plan in the first place. The investor must stick with the plans for both buying and selling. They must not sell stocks that they didn't originally plan to, and they must also buy stocks that they did plan to. Regardless of market activity, the investor should still stick to their investing goals. Instead of holding back on new investments, the investor should stick to their original plan. Good habits must be formed, and the investor must not slack off despite possible obstacles. For some activities, flexibility is important. For stock, though, sticking to the plan is much more important for ensuring success.

The investor must not change their portfolio based on recent market activities. This can prove to be quite difficult, especially in a bear market. However, it is usually worth it to stick through the hard times and wait for another period of growth. One's portfolio should be managed and properly rebalanced as necessary. Although it may be tempting to change this based on market conditions, the investor must hold out through the rough times. If investing for the long-term, the investor must ensure that the investments are, indeed, kept for the long-term.

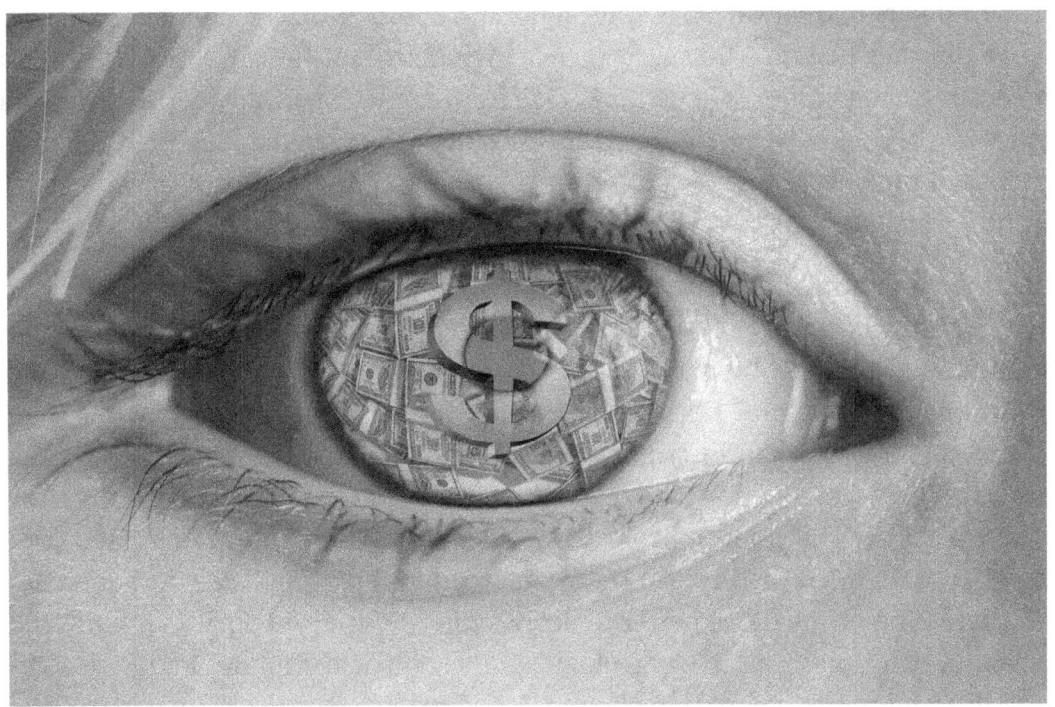

Trading Psychology

The psychology that goes into trading encompasses several factors. The trader must be able to control their emotions, make quick decisions, and remain disciplined. Of course, this is in addition to being able to understand companies and predict the direction in which the stock will go. With enough practice and research, anyone can master the technical side of trading. It's those who master the psychological side that is truly successful in trading. This is what separates the good traders from the great traders. Trading psychology can be a skill crafted by practice, but it also requires the trader to shift their way of thinking.

Traders must understand the emotions that go into trading. By first understanding them, they will allow themselves to become more skillful in the way they handle such emotions. Traders must realize that fear is a natural response to bad news about the stock market. It is natural that traders will feel a sense of urgency and be tempted to liquidate their holdings, reduce risk, or otherwise sell their stocks. This, at the time, seems to be a wise move. However, traders must make decisions quickly that will benefit them in the long term, not satisfy their emotions in the short-term. By doing so, they may risk losses, but they will not miss out on the gains that they otherwise would miss out on had they given in to their emotions. It is important for traders to realize that fear stems from what people believe is a threat to them. In this instance, the threat is to their money. Traders must recognize what is making them fearful and what the best way of dealing with that fear is. It is important to come up with a plan for what to do in hypothetical scenarios before they actually occur. What is the best way to deal with a certain outcome of stock x? Traders must answer such questions before they occur so that they have a logical look at the situation. If they wait until it actually occurs, their minds will be foggy due to the emotions they feel. They may also change the way they perceive such occurrences. Instead of viewing a drop in the price of the stock as a loss, it may be viewed as a temporary dip before further growth will occur. This shift of mindset is crucial for adopting positive trading habits.

In addition to overcoming fear, investors must know how to overcome greed. If an investor holds onto a winning stock for too long, trying to get every possible amount of money they can, these gains may quickly turn to losses. Holding onto a stock for too long can prove to be less profitable than one may imagine. Yet again, traders must come up with a plan ahead of time. They must know when the right time to let go of a stock is. At the time, it seems like a wise move to the investor. They may earn more, do better than they originally thought, and make more gains. This sometimes occurs. Most of the time, however, greed is not the right choice. Traders must distinguish between greed and making wise decisions based on market changes. Sometimes, it is better to stray from the original plan. What often occurs, however, is that emotion interferes with logic, and the investor makes an unwise move by listening to their heart instead of their head.

Investors must create an extensive plan and set rules for themselves. Instead of "going with the flow," it's important to have a step-by-step plan for the investor's trading endeavors. This should be based on rational decisions, not spur-of-the-moment emotions or instincts. They must plan out when they will enter a trade and when they will exit a trade. This must be followed no matter what, and this is a great way to eliminate emotional bias. The trader may plan for certain occurrences. If unpredictable earnings occur, whether positive or negative, the trader may establish exceptions to their plan should these occur. The trader may buy a security if certain macroeconomic events occur. They may also set limits to eliminate fear and greed. These should be upper and lower limits. The upper limits will eliminate greed, and the lower will limit fear. If such a limit is reached, the trader may stop their activities for the day to eliminate emotions from taking over their activities.

Traders must also not let regret get in the way. What is in the past is in the past. It is beneficial to recognize potential mistakes, but they should not get in the way of one's performance. Perhaps the trader regrets keeping their investment for the time period that they did. Perhaps they regret the stocks that they chose. No matter what the trader could have done, it does not matter. What matters is that they use this knowledge to improve themselves in the future. This means that the next time, they may conduct more research than they did this time.

On the other hand, traders should not rationalize their mistakes. Although it is important to not dwell on the past and all of the possible ways that the trader messed up in, the trader should still recognize that they made mistakes. This is important for self-improvement, as there will always be ways in which the trader could have conducted their trades more efficiently or effectively. As a result, the trader should definitely analyze what did go wrong every time period that they wish to do so. This will make the trader better and improve their future performance and decision-making skills.

Investing Mindset

Traders may also learn different mindsets from other traders. By researching extensively and hearing how other people conduct their trades, there is much to learn. By increasing knowledge, the investor may decrease their negative emotional reactions. They will further understand the stock market and how it operates, and this will help to eliminate such reactions.

Although it is important to stick to one's plan, traders must adopt flexible mindsets. They must be willing to try new tools, buy and sell new stocks, research new companies, and trade differently. There is no "correct" way to trade. There are simply many different ways of doing so. Some may be more profitable than others. Some may work well for one trader and not well for another. Traders should be willing to slightly experiment to see what the best way for them to trade is. This may also decrease emotion when it comes to stock.

Investors should also be critical of themselves and view their trading from a logical stance. There will be certain ways to trade that will result in greater returns. Traders must be willing to reflect on their performance and see what resulted in gains and what didn't. There is always room for improvement, and traders must recognize that. Perhaps for one time period, the trader wasn't researching as thoroughly and missed certain aspects that they should have spent more time on. Perhaps the trader did let emotion influence their trades.

Chapter 24: Tips for Becoming a Successful Top Trader

It is important to determine your personalized trading plan. Create a plan. The fact of the matter is that there is simply no way you can expect to be successful in the long term when it comes to day trading if you don't have a plan that has been personalized based on your very own strengths and weaknesses. Finding a generalized trading plan online may probably be the fastest way to start trading as soon as possible.

Determine Your Current Level of Skill

In order to ensure that you create a plan with a realistic chance for success, the first thing that you are going to want to do is determine what your current competencies are when it comes to trading, in general, as well as the underlying asset you are hoping to focus on specifically.

The more experience you have, the more elaborate and ambitious your plan can be, but it is important to determine your level of experience honestly as overestimating your experience is only going to make it more difficult for you to start turning a profit in the first place. During this step, you are also going to want to catalog your general strengths and weaknesses as they relate to trading in general and options trading specifically. It is especially important to be honest with yourself when it comes to your strengths and weaknesses, especially when it comes to your ability to maintain your composure when properly, your emotions are running high. Remember, this isn't a test that you can either pass or fail; it is simply an examination of the ways you can be the most effective trader possible. As such, if you fudge the results, then the only person who is going to be losing out is you. With enough forethought, you can maximize your strengths and minimize your weaknesses, leading to overall greater success in both the short and the long term.

Decide How Much Risk Is Right for You

When it comes to determining how much risk is the right amount, the final solution is going to be different for each trader. This is because there is no singular amount of risk that is perfect for everyone; the risk is more individualized than that. To get started figuring out the perfect amount of risk for you, the first thing that you will want to do is to determine how much capital you are going to allot solely to trading, as well as what that amount means to you. If you have saved a few thousand dollars in a month or so to give something new a try, then your overall risk is going to be little. If you saved that same amount over nearly a year of dedicated saving, then that same amount might represent a much higher risk. Regardless, it is important never to put more into a single trade than you can ever afford to lose. A good rule of thumb is that each individual trade should encompass no more than 5 percent of your total options trading fund to ensure that a small mistake doesn't end up costing you dearly. What's more, when it comes to deciding to take chances on potential trades you are only going to want to pull the trigger when you have a reasonable suspicion that the trade in question is going to end with you making three times as much in profit as what you originally put in prior to paying any related fees. To determine this amount, all you need to do is take the potential payout and divide it by the buy-in amount; if the result is greater than three, then you can move ahead with the trade with a clean conscience. This advice is what is known as the risk/reward ratio, and it is key to trading in options successfully. Besides the financial realities of your situation, you are also going to need to consider how much time you ultimately plan on spending concentrating on options trading to the exclusion of all else along with the amount of profit you hope to see in the process.

If, after determining the amount of time you hope to spend trading your financial estimates aren't as high as you might like, you can then either change the amount of time you are planning to spend or the amount of risk you are willing to put up with, there are only these three variables to work with. Be wary when it comes to raising your risk too high as major amounts of risk are as likely to lead to major losses as they are too major windfalls.

Prepare Yourself

Ideally, you will be spending the early hours of the day reading up on the likely state of the market for the moment when it opens so that you can take advantage of your planning as much as possible. As such, when it comes to creating your plan, it is important to understand how much time you realistically have to commit to maximizing your trade advantage and what other parts of your life are going to interfere with this preparation.

There is certainly money to be made by trading options at less regular hours, but the only way that you will be prepared to do so is if you know about the discrepancy ahead of time and work to minimize its impact as much as possible. In addition to the daily preparations that will be required of you, you will also need to be aware of various important due dates, both for your underlying asset of choice as a whole, as well as any holdings you might have specifically. Earnings reports of all types are sure to have a noticeable effect on the market, and if you are caught unaware, you have no choice but to take a loss that, in many cases, can be quite serious. You will also need to be aware of when any dividend payments are coming due for any options that are related to stocks that you might own. Owning an option does not entitle you to a dividend, so you must know when to exercise your options if you hope to maximize your profits at all times.

Understand When You Will Want to Get While the Getting Is Good

When it comes to creating a successful strategy, it is important that you take the time to determine exactly when you are going to want to exit every trade that you make, no matter what. Choosing this point means considering your acceptable level of risk and will ultimately serve to limit your losses, though also doing the same to your profits. Specifically, this means that when scenarios arise such as when a stock drops out of the money from a previously profitable position, you will always want to be realistic about the situation and understand that the best thing to do is to sell rather than to wait for it come back around, risking even greater losses in the interim. This logic is flawed, and what's worse, will lead to future negative habits if you are lucky enough for it to work out in your favor the first time as it will always result in a loss in the long run. Instead, you will want to determine what the best strategy is for you and your holdings based on numerous personal factors, including other trades you are currently pursuing, what you believe to be an acceptable level of risk and how closely you plan to micromanage each individual trade. Essentially, what this means is that the specific details behind the exit strategy that you choose don't matter, what does matter is that you plan out what it is going to be, before you make your first move, and then stick with it no matter what, even if every emotional cell in your being is telling you to change horses midstream and do something that is almost certainly stupid.

To keep your losses to a minimum, you are going to want to use what is known as stop losses. Stop losses are a way to automatically buy or sell options based on a predetermined set of specifications. As such, they are not terribly useful when it comes to trading in options that are likely to move a great deal in both directions over a short period of time but can be extremely useful in other, more stable situations. It doesn't matter if you are the holder or the writer, stop losses are a must for everyone involved in the interaction. You will also find that secondary stop orders are also useful when it comes to securing a predetermined amount of profit while still ensuring that you can take advantage of any ongoing positive trends as well. This is done thanks to what is known as a price target, which is the amount you feel is realistic to expect to make from the trade in question. You then simply set your first stop loss at this point and then set a second stop loss much higher. This way, when the first level of profit is reached, you can sell off half of your holdings while still retaining the rest in case the positive trend continues in a big way.

Find the Right Place to Start

Once you know when you are going to get out of any trade that you place, the next thing that you will need to consider is the right time to capitalize on the trend of a specific option.

The best way to go about doing this is to consider the amount of risk that you deem acceptable before considering what type of purchase you want to make when you come across an option that meets your criteria for purchase based on your earnings goals and your risk assessment. As a new options trader, what you are going to be the most interested in is making a single option purchase per trade. While this might not seem like a lot, it is important to keep in mind that each option is going to be worth 100 shares, which means that it only takes a little bit of movement from the underlying asset to cause significant gains or losses for any trades that you make. This means that you are going to want to be discerning when it comes to choosing the right entry point, one that is relaxed enough to ensure that you aren't waiting days between trades and strict enough that every option you come across doesn't automatically qualify.

Make Sure That Your Goals Are S.M.A.R.T.

It is important to ultimately consider what goals you have for trading and how likely each trade is to help move you one step closer to achieving them. A good way to do so is to determine if each of your goals related to options trading is not only realistic but SMART. The first SMART goal that you set should be one that is at the same time straightforward enough to more or less ensure your success while at the same time being relevant enough to your day to day life that actually succeeding will be a moment that you can easily recall in the future when success on a future goal is not nearly so assured. This way, you will start

Conclusion

Many people do not see the results that they're hoping to get just because they don't apply the tips and tricks provided to them. It is essential for you to exercise everything you learn, as that is how you will succeed in your future endeavors. Nonetheless, the topics we talked about will help you to not only become good at stock investing but to take you to the next level. Even though this book has been geared toward beginner investors, advanced people can still reap the benefits of this book.

Making money on stocks doesn't have to be a big mystery. It doesn't have to be a gamble. By being clear on what your needs are as well as the trading strategies available to you, you can put together a plan of action that can help you mix successful trades, not just once in a while, but basically every single time. Trading takes many forms, and it is dynamic as well. Times change, and with the change, markets and operational methods also change. With the advent of computers, it was logical that trading would become better and faster. This came to pass, and traders now have the capacity to trade on the go and use programs that make trading easier.

One of the best methods to use to run trades with more confidence is Algorithmic trading. This makes use of mathematical calculations to help you predict trading actions. When you do this, you eliminate various errors, including the emotional aspect of trading that tends to affect the outcome of trades. Success is all about knowing when to place a trade, how much you need to invest, and the right platform to use for trading.

While you can come up with your own system, it takes time, and the best way can be going for a ready-made system that gives you the capability you are looking for. Most of the systems give you a trial period that you can explore before you make the decision to take it up or not.

Finally, we looked at back testing. Back testing is an ideal way to use historical data to come up with assumptions about the future. Since you are using facts to determine the future, you stand to reduce many errors in future trades.

It all boils down to the learning curve, and you have to stick to this learning curve. You have to basically learn what you need to learn and take the necessary risks until you get the hang of it. Put in another way; if it were very easy, then everybody would be a billionaire. Obviously, that's not the case. You have to stick to it, and you need to put in the time to learn what you need to learn to develop enough expertise to at least trade profitably consistently.

Profitable trading, of course, means more than break even. Whether it's a dollar or hundreds of thousands of dollars, it's up to you. I wish you nothing but the highest abundance and success in your trading. Good Luck and Happy Trading!

www.ingramcontent.com/pod-product-compliance
Lightning Source LLC
Chambersburg PA
CBHW080500220526
45465CB00006B/2325